Guided Listening

A framework for using read-aloud and other oral language
experiences to build comprehension skills and help students
record, share, value, and interpret ideas

LISA DONOHUE

Pembroke Publishers Limited

© 2007 Pembroke Publishers
538 Hood Road
Markham, Ontario, Canada L3R 3K9
www.pembrokepublishers.com

Distributed in the U.S. by Stenhouse Publishers
480 Congress Street
Portland, ME 04101-3400
www.stenhouse.com

We acknowledge the financial support of the Government of Canada through the Book Publishing Industry Development Program (BPIDP) for our publishing activities.

We acknowledge the assistance of the OMDC Book Fund, an initiative of the Ontario Media Development Corporation.

Library and Archives Canada Cataloguing in Publication

Donohue, Lisa
    Guided listening / Lisa Donohue.

Includes index.
ISBN 978-1-55138-219-7

    1. Oral reading—Study and teaching (Elementary) 2. Reading comprehension—Study and teaching (Elementary) I. Title.

LB1573.5.D65 2007   372.45'2   C2007-904160-4

Editor: Kat Mototsune
Cover design: John Zehethofer
Typesetting: Jay Tee Graphics

Printed and bound in Canada
9 8 7 6 5 4 3 2 1

Contents

Acknowledgments

Thank you to the teachers and professionals who have explored the area of comprehension strategies before me, the work of Debbie Miller (*Reading With Meaning*, 2002) and Harvey and Goudvis (*Strategies That Work*, 2000), as well as others on whose work this book is based.

Thanks to Antonella Meleca for the boundless resources, creative input, and supportive encouragement; to Carol Matsoo, for your ongoing mentorship, friendship, and truly valued advice; to Nancy Mueller for your amazing teaching partnership and commitment to the profession that we share; to Dina Fabian for your continued encouragement and your belief that this book could truly happen; and to Heather Sears for sharing your understanding of metacognitive strategies with me. Thanks to the teachers who willingly explored Guided Listening with their classes and provided work samples: Helen Kurtzman, MaryLou Gilio, Peter Bonnah, Heidi Israelson, Lorraine Baillie, Tina Mauti, Maria Murgida, Saeeda Ahmed, and Daniella Giordano. Thanks to the students who eagerly completed samples to contribute to this publication, especially to my fantastic Grade 3 students, whose love for reading permeates everything they do.

Thank you, Anne Poretta, for the gentle nudge into publication; and thank you, Patricia Brooker, for sharing *the secret* with me.

Thanks to Kat Mototsune, my brilliant editor! Your endless hand-holding, guidance, and creative input were invaluable as we moved from a concept to a final publication. Thanks to Mary Macchiusi for seeing potential in a cover letter, a new instructional strategy, and pile of black line masters. The writing process has never been so real, purposeful, and enjoyable as it was while working with you.

Most importantly, thank you to my family, who had to endure countless nights listening to various segments of this book; piles of notes, books, papers, and student samples in every room; and the other inconveniences that come with putting together a book together. Thanks, Mike, for encouraging me with this book from beginning to end. I apologize for the number of times you had to unearth your bed from a mountain of books and piles of papers. I appreciate your never-ending cheerleading, nurturing, and understanding. Thanks for filling in for me in all of the areas I neglected as I took time out to write this book. Thanks to my children, Matthew and Hailey, for sharing me with all of the other children in my life. Thank you to my parents, who were greatly appreciated as they eagerly jumped in to fill any necessary need—from childcare to buying printer ink.

Finally, thanks to all of the teachers, librarians, and educators who saw value in Guided Listening and thought it was worth a try.

Introduction

"You cannot teach today's students with yesterday's materials and expect them to have success tomorrow."

—*Rhonda Stonecipher*

Imagine opening the cover of a thousand-piece jigsaw puzzle. As you gaze into the confusion of colors and shapes, lines and textures, you know that somehow these smaller pieces amazingly all belong together. Each piece fills a unique place to create a larger image. However, as you stare into the mosaic of pieces before you, the final image is invisible. What would you do if there was no picture on the cover of the box? Where would you begin? How would you start to organize those pieces so that they would all fit together? Imagine, now, that you knew that the red pieces formed an apple at the centre of a bowl of fruit. Would this change your approach to organizing the pieces before you? Perhaps you would begin by sorting through the pieces and selecting only the red pieces that would combine to form the apple. Somehow, having an idea of the final image helps us to organize the smaller components in a way that makes sense.

Guided Listening is based on the principle that students listen more effectively when given a purpose for listening. Students are bombarded with so many ideas that it is sometimes challenging for them to see the unified purpose of text—the bigger picture the ideas represent. When given the tools to organize this collection of ideas (like the picture on a puzzle box), they can listen attentively for cues and have a greater focus for their listening.

On a recent vacation in the southwestern United States, we found ourselves driving south along a beautiful coastal highway. On our right there were spectacular ocean views of crashing waves and sandy beaches. To our left there were breathtaking cliffs and crumbling hills, with the land majestically bowing to meet the sea. Suddenly, ahead of us the highway divided and branched inland. We continued along this route for a number of kilometres before the view became mundane and we wished to return to the ocean views of the coastal highway. A crossroad appeared ahead; it seemed to be a main throughway. We decided to follow this unknown route, believing that if we headed west, we would again find the ocean. It was not long before the town faded into the distance and a sharp left turn led us into the mountains. The road was winding and narrow. On the right the road dropped sharply into unknown abysses. The path ahead seemed uncertain as it wound perilously close to the edge of high mountains and around bends. As almost all signs of civilization disappeared behind us, we questioned whether or not it was wise to continue along this road.

We were like children listening to an onslaught of ideas, thoughts, and images, trying to decipher the important concepts and decide whether or not to persevere. How many times have you seen your students cock their heads sharply to the side, furrow their brows, and try to decode new material?

Let's return to the example of the highway journey. Did we proceed? The key to our success was the roadmap that clearly marked the path to follow. Knowing that the coastal highway was ahead instilled in us the confidence to persevere through the unknown and to emerge at the desired destination. We were not sure how we would get there, but we knew where we were going.

Guided Listening is a roadmap for students, with the destination clearly marked. When they know their final destination, they are more able to recognize the landmarks along the way.

1

What is Guided Listening?

"The mind arranges and stores information in an orderly fashion. New information about a concept is filed into an existing framework of categories called a schema that contains specific information about a concept. So, when prior knowledge is retrieved, this schema provides a framework on which to attach new knowledge"

—*Karen Bromley*

Guided Listening is an instructional tool that effectively links elements of oral language with independent reading through the use of metacognitive strategies. Through Guided Listening, students become more proficient at understanding that reading is a "dialogue with text." Guided Listening creates the scaffold for effective listening. Students listen more effectively when they clearly understand what they are listening for. Guided Listening establishes this through giving students

- a purpose for listening
- a framework on which to organize their ideas
- a way to record, share, and value the ideas of others
- a practical transfer of these skills to their independent work

Guided Listening vs. the Traditional Read-Aloud

Most teachers read daily to their students as an essential component of the balanced literacy program.

Often while I was reading to my class, I would wonder if their minds were wandering off. Sometimes I even caught my own mind straying from the words on the page, yet the automatic reading aloud continued. Sometimes I saw my students doodling, fidgeting, or playing with items of their clothing (or the clothing of others). I sometimes saw raised hands and, hopeful that they may have something profound to add to the story, was disappointed when I discovered that they needed to go to the washroom. On occasion, I would complete a story, and then proceed to have a "discussion" with the students about why a character did something, or what they would have done in a similar situation—often to be faced with students unable to recall the intricate details of the text, or even the overall theme. *How about providing proof from the text? How do you know that? What made you think that?* They were often unable to recall the specific details of the text or had not attended to the things that were truly important.

I was once surprised after reading a chapter of *Charlotte's Web* by E.B. White that, when I asked my students to describe the main idea, and they told me that Fern had a crush on Henry Fussy.

I wondered if my students would be able to listen more effectively if they understood the purpose for listening *before* I read to them. If we give the students the "questions" ahead of time, then they can listen for the answers, instead of trying to remember random bits of information that may possibly be the answer to a possible question that the teacher may possibly ask that they may possibly have to answer.

Guided Listening is not an "add-on," not simply something to add into your instructional day. Guided Listening allows you to take instructional activities that are already in place and make them more successful, purposeful, and focused. Every teacher reads aloud to the class, and every teacher allows time in the day for independent reading. Guided Listening allows these two activities to become purposefully connected. Incorporating Guided Listening to your teaching practice is a natural transition. It gives structure to already existing practices and results in invaluable assessment opportunities that can serve to strengthen students' learning.

What Does a Traditional Read-Aloud Look Like?

- The teacher sits with the class to read aloud a text to them.
- The students gather together to sit and listen to the story and look at the pictures.
- The teacher pauses occasionally to discuss concepts and ideas with the students.
- The teacher poses questions for students to answer.
- Students may be asked to share their thinking; one or two answers may be shared with the class.
- There may be a follow-up activity after reading the text, for which students are asked to remember, retell, and reflect on parts of what they have heard.
- The teacher usually focuses on incidental learning, reading the text and thinking-aloud to model successful reading strategies.
- There is little or no assessment of students' understanding of the text.

What Does Guided Listening Look Like?

- The teacher gathers the class together to share the text with them using the Guided Listening procedure.
- The teacher shares with the class the purpose for listening and provides focused instruction *prior* to reading the text.
- Students use clipboards to record their ideas while listening.
- The teacher pauses occasionally to discuss specific concepts and ideas with the students.
- The students pose questions, present ideas, make inferences/predictions/connections, and reflect on the ideas of their peers
- All students are actively engaged in the listening task.
- There is individual student accountability for learning.
- There can be direct connection to, and transfer of, listening skills to independent reading.
- Isolation of listening and reading strategies allow opportunities for practice and mastery of skills.
- Guided Listening allows the teacher opportunities for instructional feedback, diagnostic assessment of student's oral language skills, and intervention as needed for specific students (diversified instruction), and isolated assessment of each listening and reading strategy.

Providing direct instruction on metacognitive reading strategies, allowing time for students to independently practice these skills, and assessing and providing feedback, results in strong readers.

Read-alouds and independent reading are essential daily components of balanced literacy program; however, students often become passive observers and not all students are accountable for demonstrating their learning or have an equal opportunity to participate in discussions. Guided Listening helps students to listen critically and respond appropriately.

- During a traditional read-aloud, the teacher is fully engaged in the text, but is unsure if all students are on task, listening attentively, and understanding the text. Guided Listening ensures that all students are engaged and accountable for recording and sharing their ideas.
- During a traditional read-aloud, the teacher asks the questions and the students answer them. During Guided Listening, students ask the questions; many questions remain unanswered.
- During a traditional read-aloud, the teacher determines which ideas are important based on questions the teacher poses for discussion; during Guided Listening, students determine important ideas from the text based on parameters set by the teacher.
- During a traditional read-aloud, the students are not aware of the follow-up task while they are listening, so they are unable to selectively listen for information that may be helpful. In Guided Listening, the students are presented with a clear and concise purpose for listening prior to the read-aloud.
- The traditional read-aloud is not usually connected to students' independent reading. Guided Listening provides a clear connection and direct transfer between the instructional purpose of the read-aloud and the student's independent reading.

Metacognition

I think; therefore I am…
I think about my thinking; therefore, I understand.

Keith Lenz (2005) from the University of Kansas concludes that the most successful ways of teaching comprehension strategies is to use very direct and explicit instruction.

Metacognition, in short, means thinking about thinking. When students are intentionally taught the processes connected with successful reading, they become successful readers themselves. It is not enough for students to know what reading strategies are connected to reading, but they need to have direct instruction and sufficient time to independently practice these skills. Students require monitoring and feedback on their use of reading strategies. Instruction on metacognitive reading strategies needs to be ongoing, purposeful, integrated into a variety of subject areas and with a variety of texts. When you teach strategies in isolation, you allow students to focus specifically on the steps associated with each skill resulting in gradual integration and independence.

Meena Singhal (2001) concluded that strategy training leads to improved reading performance. A chart that summarizes her recommendations for successful strategy instruction is on page 12.

Successful Strategy Instruction	Connections to Guided Listening
Teachers must focus on the processes involved in reading and allocate instructional time to teaching these strategies through direct strategy-instruction and modelling.	Guided Listening is a structured time with direct instruction and modelling of each metacognitive listening strategy.
Teachers must think about how a particular strategy is best applied and in which context.	Texts should be carefully selected so that students will easily be able to apply the strategy that is being taught.
Teachers should monitor use of reading strategies in order to determine individual students' strengths and needs. This, in turn, will help to provide effective and appropriate strategy instruction.	Students' application of oral language can be monitored during Guided Listening. This easily forms the basis for further instruction.
Teachers must present strategies as purposeful to a variety of texts and contexts so that students can apply these strategies in a variety or reading situations.	Using a variety of texts for Guided Listening will help students to effectively transfer their skills and knowledge of listening strategies to a variety of applications. Introducing students to different forms of media will also facilitate this transfer of skills.
Strategy instruction needs to be consistent and ongoing, not just a single lesson or unit.	Using Guided Listening on a regular basis helps students to continue to build on previous knowledge and begin to use these strategies with greater ease and integration.
Students must be provided with opportunities to practice strategies that they have been taught.	Encouraging students to read independently immediately following a read-aloud enables them to relate listening strategies to reading strategies, and to practice the application of strategies while they are fresh in their mind.
Students benefit from sharing with each other about their reading strategies.	Encouraging students to share their thoughts and ideas during Guided Listening gives them the chance to verbalize their thoughts. Sometimes, students think better when they can "hear themselves think." Sharing with partners or groups helps to strengthen their learning.

Using Advance Organizers

Mayer (2003) concluded that students who received a diagram before listening to a passage had greater retention of the material.

The idea of using advance organizers is not a new one. Originally proposed by David Ausubel (1960), it is believed to increase the learning and retention of new information. Ausubel suggested that learning becomes meaningful when integrated into a child's existing knowledge base. The most important element in learning is not how information is presented, but how the new information is integrated into an existing knowledge base. Students learn better when they have previewed information. Teachers could do this by providing a brief introduction about the information before beginning the lesson.

Although Guided Listening makes use of advance organizers, they are different in nature and purpose than those suggested by Ausubel. The advance organizers of Guided Listening provide students with cues as to which strategies they must use in order to effectively interpret and utilize the information. Students are presented with an outline of listening strategies that help to create a purpose for listening, to focus their attention and critically analyze relevant information.

By providing advance organizers that focus students' attention on one specific metacognitive strategy at a time, you give students the means to narrow the amount of information they are hearing and to determine which parts are most relevant to the task at hand. Practicing the strategies helps students to become fluent with each strategy in isolation, eventually leading to them internalizing and integrating these strategies into their personal schemas. When students automatically listen critically, analyze and synthesize information, and make inferences and predictions while listening, they will easily transfer these skills to their independent reading. Developing critical listening skills helps students to develop stronger metagcognitive skills, as well as to better understand their own reading strengths and needs.

2

Why Guided Listening?

"It is not true that we have only one life to live; if we can read, we can live as many more lives and as many kinds of lives as we wish."

—*S.I. Hayakawa*

"Upon our children—how they are taught—rests the fate—or fortune—of tomorrow's world."
—*B. C. Forbes*

One of the main focuses of Guided Listening is student acquisition and use of listening and reading skills:

- Guided Listening provides focused instruction and independent practice, allowing students to become proficient at identifying and applying metacognitive listening and reading strategies.
- Providing students with a framework for organizing their thoughts helps them to activate their existing knowledge and efficiently process new ideas.
- Students become independently proficient at each strategy by using them in isolation. This leads to the natural progression of the integration of all metacognitive strategies.
- Consistent assessment of students' learning allows teachers to provide students with regular feedback and to guide further instruction.
- Guided Listening provides purposeful instruction for read-alouds and independent reading, naturally linking the two.
- Through Guided Listening, students become more competent readers, as they begin to think about what they are thinking as they read.

Classroom Connections

Transfer of Skills to Independent Reading

In the Guided Listening process, many of the prompts for independent reading are very similar to the prompts from the read-aloud. This way, the instructions remain the same and students can focus their attention on their text, rather than interpreting the instructions.

The direct transfer of skills from read-aloud to independent reading is clear. If you clearly guide and model the use of comprehension strategies, and then provide an immediate opportunity for students to try it out on their own, you scaffold their success. Students are very comfortable with familiarity, and knowing that they have just done a task successfully gives them the confidence to try it on their own.

It is very important to monitor students while they are reading independently. At first, it is crucial to observe students reading behaviors, to redirect when necessary, and to clarify any misconceptions. As students become more comfortable with the expectations and routines of Guided Listening, their independence will expand.

Connections to Guided Reading

Guided Listening provides the natural link between read-aloud and independent reading. Teaching each comprehension strategy in isolation and building on student's existing knowledge allows you to be aware of each student's strengths and needs. Some students will master the strategies faster than others, and some may require further guidance to become comfortable with their use. Regularly reviewing student work as they practice the varying strategies will give you direction for further instruction. Looking at the way students explain their thinking, both while listening and while reading, will give you a great deal of insight into the students' individual strengths and needs. Using this assessment to further guide instruction is the next logical step.

When you can analyze the strengths and needs of the class, it becomes very easy to form smaller groups for guided reading. For example, it may be obvious that three students are struggling with Asking Questions; you may decide to use small group instruction. When these students are placed together, it becomes possible for them to have direct instruction and guided practice to develop the particular skill. Furthermore, if a group of students excel at making connections, then this might serve as the structure for smaller group instruction. Perhaps they can examine a series of articles on a similar topic or short texts by the same author. Guided reading groups should be fluid and constantly changing as the students' needs evolve. Using assessment from Guided Listening to form these groups makes these reorganizations easy and purposeful.

Reading for Enjoyment

"If you have to write every time you read, it sucks the fun out of reading."

It is fantastic to see students actively engaged in a text, whispering to each other their ideas, and having "ah-ha" moments as they piece together important clues from a story.

Reading for entertainment is very different from reading for learning. I wholeheartedly agree that, to become an effective reader, one must love reading; however, to truly love reading, one must be effective at it. Helping kids understand the metacognitive processes involved in reading provides them with insight into their thoughts as readers.

Although Guided Listening is a valuable tool in the classroom, there are times when the strategy lesson is to "enjoy the book." Once a class has become familiar with the strategies, and can use them with ease, it is interesting to present students with the task of listening for enjoyment. If students are proficient at using the comprehension strategies, they will automatically revert to responding in familiar ways: jumping in with connections; hopping from leg to leg, eager to share their predictions; whispering to each other their inferences; and bursting to share their visualizations. These positive conversations about texts are possible only with a firm foundation.

Students should not have to write every time they read; however, until they've internalized the comprehension processes connected with effective reading, actively involving them provides focused purposeful instruction while they read or listen. Before I began teaching with Guided Listening, students were usually passive observers during a read-aloud, now I can't seem to get through a page without having them jump in to explain their thinking and comment on the ideas of others. Students are fully engaged, not only with the ideas from the book, but with their own ideas and the ideas of others. Who is having more fun reading: the passive observer or the active participant?

Note-Taking

I remember a beautiful September morning, as I filed into the university auditorium with hundreds of keen, bright-eyed first-year students. As the professor took his place behind the lectern, I removed an arsenal of pens from my backpack. I sat poised, pen at the ready to record each and every idea that should waft through the muffled sound system and reach my ears. Each and every idea? Yes, indeed. I made it my personal mission to record each and every word spoken—in longhand. I scribbled feverishly, recording sentence after sentence, page after page of copious notes. After three hours, I neatly piled the stack of double-sided manuscripts into my backpack, massaged my right hand, and set out for the next class. During my first year I wished for the gift of ambidexterity—I would have double the opportunity to create transcripts for my classes. As I struggled to master the art of note-taking, it became abundantly clear that I had never really been taught how to decipher important ideas and record them effectively.

We often expect students to arrive in the higher grades able to take notes. However, little time is dedicated in earlier grades to teaching this critical skill. Note-taking is essential, as students move through high school and onto college, university, or other aspects of life.

This skill, like all others, needs to be taught in small increments that students are able to master. If this instruction starts early, in the primary grades, students will learn the essential skills of note-taking. Guided Listening provided the initial instructions for students to begin to develop these skills. By setting a purpose for listening and a framework on which to organize ideas, it gives students practice at listening critically, filtering out unnecessary information, and summarizing key ideas. If we encourage students to record their thinking in creative ways (using graphic organizers, diagrams, illustrations, words or phrases) they will begin to create their own style of short-hand.

Strengthening Oral Language Skills

Oral communication skills are essential. Encouraging students to play a more interactive role in their learning is a necessary transition in current education. Learning is not a passive act, but takes engagement, questioning, and discussion in order for it to truly be effective. Providing frequent brief opportunities for students to have focused sharing times with partners allows them to quickly formulate and articulate their ideas.

Throughout Guided Listening activities, teachers should pause frequently and encourage students to share their thinking with a partner (brief pauses of 30 seconds or less). For example, while reading, the teacher may pause and say: "This is really exciting, I wonder what will happen next." Rather than asking students to raise their hands and choosing one or two students to tell the class, the teacher will find it much more effective if he/she encourages students to turn to a partner and make a prediction. This allows all students to share their ideas and know that they have been heard. After such a pause, students quickly return to being fully engaged in learning, curious to know about the text, and their attention is easily refocused. As students become familiar with these types of

When it becomes necessary to redirect students to active listening, it works well to encourage them to "finish their thought" rather than "stop talking."

interactive pauses, they will quickly learn to share their thinking and then refocus to continue with the book.

Students who are given frequent opportunities to share their thinking find it easier to articulate their ideas, integrate new ideas into their thinking, and value, respect, and listen to the ideas of others.

Listening to and Valuing the Ideas and Opinions of Others

Thinking with a friend not only provides students the opportunity to express their ideas in words, but encourages them to hear the ideas of others. Knowing that their ideas have been heard, students feel that their thoughts have been validated and they become more accountable for their learning. It is important that students have the skills to respond to the ideas and opinions of others. Courteous listening behaviors, mutual respect, and thoughtful questioning are all effective interactive listening skills that students need to see modelled regularly and to have numerous opportunities to practice. Students also need to actively listen to their peers, wait their turn when speaking, and demonstrate genuine interest in the ideas of others. These values of respectful listening and sharing can be strengthened through regular opportunities for interactions and positive modelling.

Listening Critically and Analyzing New Information

During Guided Listening, students will have two areas upon which to focus their listening. Directly, they listen to the teacher and the text from which the lesson is being learned; indirectly, students listen to their peers as they share their learning with each other. In both instances, students will need to draw on their personal experiences and knowledge to critically analyze new information.

Given that mutual respect is of utmost importance, students learn that it is acceptable to disagree—but it must be done respectfully. Steamrolling a partner with their own ideas does not foster an environment for positive learning.

When listening to the text, students may use background knowledge to contribute to their understanding of the text. When listening to their peers, students will also listen critically in order to analyze and evaluate their thinking. In this way, students will use their personal knowledge, information from the text, and their own ideas to evaluate and consider the ideas of their peers. As students weigh the information from a variety of sources, they may formulate new ideas integrating learning from these sources.

3

Listening Strategies Become Reading Strategies

"The way a book is read—which is to say, the qualities a reader brings to a book—can have as much to do with its worth as anything the author puts into it."

—Norman Cousins

The work of Debbie Miller (2002) and Harvey and Goudvis (2000) identify seven metacognitive reading strategies. These include Making Inferences, Making Predictions, Determining Important Information, Making Connections, Visualizing, Asking Questions, and Synthesizing. Palinscar and Ransom (1988), Brown et al (1986), and Paris, Lipson and Wixon (1983) found that, in addition to understanding these strategies, students must know when, why, and how to use them. Direct modelling of these strategies with texts followed immediately by guided practice will help student to understand these strategies and become proficient at applying them to both listening and reading.

Making Inferences and Predictions

Inferring and predicting are closely linked skills. Both require the student to attend to information in the text and draw upon their own knowledge to form a guess about the text. Harvey and Goudvis (2000) state

> Predicting is related to inferring, of course, but we predict outcomes, events, or actions that are confirmed or contradicted by the end of the story. Inferences are often more open-ended and may remain unresolved when the story draws to a close.

Identifying Theme

Inferring is often used when identifying the theme of a story. If students are told to listen critically for the theme, moral, or lesson in a story, they are able to filter through the erroneous information and break the story into its most rudimentary elements.

A favorite author for this activity is Dr. Seuss, as many of his works have very simple underlying themes that are easily decoded by critical listeners. For example, *Horton Hatches the Egg* tells the story of an irresponsible bird (Mayzie) who would much rather have fun than take care of her egg. She cons poor Horton, an elephant, to sit in her tree in her place. Mayzie then flies off for an

Another such story by Dr. Seuss is *The Sneetches*. If students are reminded of the importance of looking beyond the obvious tale of strange-looking birds (Sneetches) some with stars on the tummies and some without, they will identify the themes of equality, acceptance, fairness, inclusion, and discrimination.

extended vacation leaving Horton to tend the egg. Horton repeatedly states, "I said what I meant, and I meant what I said, an elephant's faithful one hundred percent." Finally Mayzie and Horton meet again, just as the egg begins to hatch. She wishes to reclaim the egg now that the hard part is over. The egg hatches to reveal an elephant-bird. Horton's faithfulness is rewarded.

On the surface, the story tells the tale of an elephant, an egg, and a bird. However, if students are told to look beyond the characters and summarize the lessons learned in this story in one sentence, they may think of such themes as responsibility, loyalty, faithfulness, deception, etc.

Prompts for Making Inferences

- What is the lesson the author wants us to learn from this book?
- What's the author's message?
- What is the theme of the book?
- What do you think it means when…?
- How do you think the characters are feeling?
- How would you feel if you were the main character?
- What did you really want to know at the end of the story?
- What conclusions can you make?
- What did you like/dislike about the book?
- How might the story have been different if one of the other characters were telling it?
- Even though it doesn't really say in the book, how did you know…?
- If you could hear another's character's point of view, who's would you like to hear? Why?

Reading Between the Lines

Reading between the lines is a more challenging inferential strategy than identifying theme. Guided Listening provides the perfect opportunity for students to be introduced to this skill. Students will find it easier to read between the lines if the teacher places emphasis on certain phrases, allows wait time for students to generate new ideas and make connections, and draws their attention to subtleties in the author's work.

Foreshadowing is a technique commonly used by authors but often missed by students. Encouraging students to recall what the author said earlier or to ponder what the author's intent was in making a certain statement may help trigger ideas for students.

A fantastic book for this type of inferencing is *The Mystery at Eatum Hall* by John Kelly. Glenda (a goose) and Horace (a hog) Pork-Fowler are invited to spend the weekend at Eatum Hall, and inn owned by Dr. Hunter (a wolf). When they arrive, no one is there to greet them, but there is plenty of food. Glenda and Horace eat gluttonously throughout the weekend; the illustrations provide hints as to Dr. Hunter's true intentions. The weekend ends with a pie-eating festival, and students are left to "read between the lines" as to the contents of the pie. Students thoroughly enjoy the task of making inferences and drawing conclusions as they listen to this story.

Understanding Characters' Feelings

As readers, we tend to connect with characters through our own experiences or emotions. Sophisticated readers are able to easily draw conclusions about how

During a Guided Listening lesson, if students are told to listen for cues that tell how a character feels, they will become more savvy at finding these clues on their own.

characters feel based on cues from the author. Younger readers sometimes require more guidance in this area. If the author does not say that someone is sad, for example, students may not realize that this is so. Directing students' attention to cues such as body language, tone of voice, or actions may help then make these inferences with greater ease.

Consider the following excerpt from *The Breadwinner* by Deborah Ellis. This story tells of the challenges faced by Parvana and her family to survive in Afghanistan under the harsh rule of the Taliban. Few students have experienced feelings of sheer terror but, using the cues provided by the author, they are able to identify Parvana's feelings.

> Parvana felt the shadow before she saw it, as the man moved between her and the sun. Turning her head, she saw the dark turban that was the uniform of the Taliban. A rifle was slung across his chest, as casually as her father's shoulder bag had been slung across hers…
> The Talib kept looking down at her. Then he put his hand inside his vest. Keeping his eyes on Parvana, he drew something out of his vest pocket.
> Parvana was about to squish her eyes shut and wait to be shot when she saw the Talib had taken out a letter.

Making Predictions

Listening to and evaluating the ideas of their peers help students to refine their own predictions and gain greater insight into the text. Many different perspectives help to create a broader image.

Students naturally like to make predictions. When given the opportunity, they will frequently have some input on what they think will happen next. The challenge, however, comes when they are asked to provide evidence for their predictions. If students are informed prior to reading aloud that there will be a point in the story where they will be asked for a prediction and evidence to support their ideas, they will be more focused while listening, mentally collecting and organizing information.

Brave Irene, a picture book by William Steig, tells the tale of a young girl, Irene, who faces insurmountable obstacles as she attempts to deliver a special gown to the duchess through a snowstorm. There are numerous opportunities for students to predict the outcome of Irene, the dress, and the dress box. Students enjoy discovering if their predictions were correct.

Prompts for Making Predictions

• What do you think will happen?
• What clues did the author give that something important is about to happen?
• What evidence did you base your prediction on?

Determining Important Ideas

The format and the genre of a text greatly influence the way we determine important ideas.

We read texts differently, depending on the type of text, the purpose with which we are reading, and the perspective we are reading from.

Compare reading a newspaper and a textbook. In neither case would you probably read the text in its entirety. When we read a newspaper, we rely heavily on the headlines, photographs, and captions to help us determine the importance of the article; when reading a textbook, we might use a table of contents, chapter titles, or an index to help us locate the information we are seeking.

Would you read a magazine in the same manner as a mystery novel? Certainly not! Novels are intended to be read sequentially, revealing pertinent information in an order dictated by the author. But you "flip" through a magazine in any direction, pausing to read an article, look at a caption, or examine a photograph as it captures our interest. You might read a magazine any number of times, identifying different key concepts each time.

Personal perspective also determines which ideas will be considered important. For example, a sports fan and a politician would definitely identify different important features when reading the same newspaper.

Prompts for Determining Important Ideas

- What ideas do you think are important?
- What does the author want us to think about?
- What do you think the story is really about?
- Why do you think the author used italics/bold/ capitals/etc. for this word/sentence?
- What is the main idea of the story? How do you know?
- What evidence supports this information?
- What are some facts about this?
- What did you learn from the text?
- What information did you initially think was important? Has that changed? Why? What do you think is important now?

As sophisticated readers, we are able to decipher between text styles and the varying approaches to them, but students need to be taught these differences. They need to recognize the differences between text formats and to identify which skills they need to determine importance. When introducing various text forms to students, it is important to model how to make sense of the information presented and how it is organized. Students need to be taught the elements of a variety of text forms so that they have a toolkit with which to attack new texts.

Non-fiction vs. Fiction

During Guided Listening, demonstrate to students how authors use features of the text to emphasize important ideas. Commenting on italics or the use of bold print, interesting punctuation or illustrations, captions or graphics helps to identify important ideas.

Many students enjoy non-fiction books, but they tend to approach them as they would a novel—they begin at the beginning and end at the end. It is helpful for teachers to model how to use a non-fiction book as a resource. Modelling to students how to use an index or table of contents to gives them "permission" to flip through a book and read only the information that they have deemed important.

When reading non-fiction, importance is usually placed on facts. Fiction may require the reader to determine important ideas, then possibly revisit, revise, and rethink the ideas that were originally deemed important. As the story unfolds, a critical reader will eliminate information that no longer seems relevant and build on ideas that seem critical to the plot. This spiral—identifying important ideas, learning more information, then revisiting initial thoughts and revising them to go on to learn more information again—is an ongoing interaction between the reader and the text. Sophisticated readers do this seamlessly, but younger readers need guidance. Asking students to determine important ideas after reading aloud a small part of a book, and then continuing to read and revisit their original ideas, helps them along this journey of refining their thinking through interaction with the text.

Making Connections

The child who says "That's just like the show I saw on TV last night!" has made a text-to-text connection.

Students make connections in three ways: Text-to-Self, Text-to-Text, and Text-to-World. Children naturally find connections between texts and their own experiences. Even toddlers looking through a picture book search their own schema for things that they recognize in print to connect to that which they have experienced. For example, a two-year-old may not know what a sheep is, but is quite familiar with dogs, so she may point to a picture of a sheep and say "dog."

This natural desire to fit the unknown into the known continues throughout our lives as readers. We are constantly interpreting text based on our personal experiences and knowledge bases. As children get a broader range of experiences with a variety of texts, they become more adept at seeing ways that they are connected. Children begin to look for connections between things they know about the world to be true and the texts they read; the statement, "That could never happen…there's no way he could jump off the top of a building and survive!" is a text-to-world connection. The student is analyzing the concept introduced in the text and comparing it with his/her knowledge of basic physics—height, gravity, and acceleration—although not in so many words.

As I greeted my new class in September, I was greeted by a family who had just arrived in Canada from Korea. Their daughter was starting a new school in a new country with a new language. The only word she knew was "Hi." As her mother wiped her tear-stained face and kissed her goodbye, we all felt her anxiety, even though she could not tell us in words. As time passed, she started to use English phrases and her skills strengthened. She would frequently try to say new words and phrases, and soon became able to understand and communicate. One day, I read the book *My Name Is Yoon* by Helen Recorvits, the story of a young girl from Korea who needs to find her place in a new country. As I read this book with my class, we were all able to make personal connections with the text. Many students recalled when they were new to a situation or a school; they were all able to relate to the feelings of Yoon. My text selection helped the students making meaningful connections based on experiences I knew they had in common with the characters in the text. Finding one's way in a new country can be an overwhelming experience. It's nice for students to connect with each other and with stories, to know that they are not alone.

Prompts for Making Connections

• Does this remind you of another story?
• Do any of the characters in the story remind you of anyone you know?
• What does this story remind you of?
• Have you had a similar experience?
• Do any of the pictures remind you of anything?
• Where have you seen/heard this before?

Strategies for Teaching Students to Make Connections

Activate Prior Knowledge

In order for students to effectively make connections while a text is being read, it is important that the teacher set the stage for the story. Prior to reading, you may wish to introduce students to the main idea of the story, the main character, or some other key element. This will allow students to begin to activate their prior knowledge in order to make connections to the text.

Allow Sufficient Wait Time

Wait time is also an important element when teaching a Guided Listening lesson on Making Connections. If we ask the students to consider a time when they felt the same as the main character, it may take students a few minutes to recall a personal experience.

Encourage Sharing Ideas With Peers

Listening to the connections made by others may trigger memories for students. Too often, teachers share their personal connections with students but neglect to leave enough time for them to share with and listen to each other.

Text Selection

When asking students to make connections, text selection is crucial. If you select books in which the characters are similar in age, interest, or situation to your students, it may increase the likelihood that they will make connections with ease. Selecting non-fiction texts on a subject that students have had some prior experience with will also help students to make connections.

Intentionally Link Books

If you use a number of texts on the same subject or by the same author, students will naturally begin to see links between the texts. It may be more difficult for students to make text-to-self connections with books on certain topics (for example; the Holocaust, or slavery), but if they have been exposed to a variety of books on the subject, they will begin to make connections between the texts and, as their knowledge base grows, they will be able to make more text-to-world connections.

Include Various Forms of Media

Remember to include movies, newspapers, magazines, TV shows, Internet sites, games, and songs as texts. These are valid text forms, and they play a very prominent role in most students' lives. Think of how much stronger a student's understanding of a fictional text would be if he is able to see connections between it and his favorite computer game.

Visualizing

When we speak of visualizing to students, we often tell them to create pictures in their mind or to imagine the story like a movie. Although it is essential for students to fully incorporate their sense of vision, their other senses are just as crucial. Visualizing with all of their senses increases students' understanding of the text. Imagining the tone of a character's voice, the smell of fresh bread baking, or the feeling the dampness in a musty old basement is a visualization skill that students need to develop. When taught visualizing through Guided Listening, students will learn to focus their attention on key phrases that help to create these mental images.

Prompts for Visualizing

- What can you picture in your mind?
- What do you think the character/setting/etc. looks like?
- If you were inside the book, what would you be able to hear/smell/taste/feel?
- What words does the author use to help us to create a picture in our mind?

The book *Poppy* by Avi presents students with countless opportunities to use all of their senses as they perceive the dangers felt by a little mouse, very alone, in a dark dangerous forest.

> There was no time to waste. She dived into the log. …she moved deeper in to the musty dark. Suddenly she stopped. At the far end of the log she heard the distinct sound of heavy breathing. It was exactly what she had feared: Another creature was already in the log. …Poppy stared back in to the log's darkness. The breathing and rattling were drawing nearer. She was trapped.
>
> In the obscure murk of the log's interior, Poppy crouched tensely. Slouching slowly out of the dark came a flat-faced beast with a blunt black snout and fierce grizzled whiskers. Its eyes were heavily lidded as though it had just awakened. The creature moved ponderously, with a waddle and rattle. Its stench was powerful enough to make Poppy clamp a paw over her nose.

When your heart races, and you can't turn the pages fast enough, then you have indeed connected with the author in a special way and are feeling the feelings of the characters. When you laugh out loud, or burst into tears—then it is because you have truly visualized the story as told by the author.

This example clearly demonstrates that visualization is much more than making a "picture" in one's mind. It is the carefully woven cues that we attend to, that stimulate all of our senses.

Participating in the anticipation of the characters, sensing the danger lurking around the next bend, or feeling the hair on the back of your arms stand up are also visualization skills. *Where the Red Fern Grows* by Wilson Rawls is a touching story of a boy and his two dogs. The selfless love between them is undeniable. As effective listeners and readers, students intricately weave images of these characters into a heart-warming tale. Without visualization, this story would fail, as the author plays on the reader's ability to see, feel, and sense the challenges and tribulations faced by the main character, Billy. Using this book for Guided Listening creates numerous opportunities for students to become proficient at using their senses to envision the story.

When listening to an excerpt like this one from *Where the Red Fern Grows*, your students will be able to attend to a variety of cues. Identify key phrases to help them form an emotional connection with the text by creating a mental image of what they might see, feel, hear, or sense if they were the main character.

In this selection, the author creates the perception of danger by alerting one to the sounds, feelings and images sensed by this young boy as he is alone in the darkness of the night.

Then I saw them—two burning, yellow eyes—staring at me from the shadowy foliage of the tree. I stopped, petrified with fear.

The deep baying of Old Dan stopped and again the silence closed in.

I stared back at the unblinking eyes.

I could make out the bulk of a large animal, crouched on a huge branch, close to the trunk of the big tree. Then it moved. I heard the scratch of razor-sharp claws on the bark. It stood up and moved out of the shadows on to the limb. I saw it clearly as it passed between the moon and me. I knew what it was. It was the devil cat of the Ozarks, the mountain lion.

Non-Fiction

Non-fiction texts sometimes present an interesting challenge for students. When working with expository texts, it is helpful for students to make connections to things that they already know about in order to visualize something they may not understand as fully.

Did you know that the blue whale's heart weighs about 1000 pounds and it has about 14,000 pounds of blood in its body? That means that its heart is about the size of a Volkswagen bug, and its aorta is so large that a human could crawl through it. (enchantedlearning.com)

As you read this to yourself, which pieces of information have that largest impact? Would you remember the exact numbers, or did you create a mental image of someone crawling through the aorta of a whale?

When reading non-fiction with students, it is important to have them listen for key connections that will help them visualize and remember important information. Using graphic organizers—such as timelines, charts, webs, Venn diagrams, idea trails, and fishbones—may help students form greater understanding of non-fiction texts. Encouraging students to record their ideas visually by drawing a diagram while they are listening is a good way for them to represent information graphically.

Asking Questions

As teachers, it is natural for us to expect to have the answers for our students' questions. The purpose of teaching students to ask questions is to allow them to have a dialogue, not with the teacher, but with the author. If we answer the questions for the students, then there is no need for them to further interact with the text.

Students may generate questions on a number of levels. At first it is challenging for students to see beyond the literal but, with practice, they become able to delve deeper into the meaning of the text and ask more substantial questions.

Some themes generate more questions than others. Books that deal with controversial subject matter, issues of injustice, or inequality leave readers questioning the very concept of the story. Books like *The Diary of Anne Frank* and *Number the Stars* by Lois Lowry, a holocaust story of Annemarie and her family as they try to help their Jewish friends escape to safety, raise a lot more questions than answers.

Students initially find it difficult to ask questions. It is not common for students to ask questions; they are accustomed to answering them. Encouraging students to share their questions and focusing attention on what makes a good question helps reshape the way they approach asking questions. When students can ask questions that initiate controversy or a debate, then they have truly mastered the art of asking questions.

Fly Away Home by Eve Bunting is a picture book for students of all ages. It tells the story of a young boy and his father who are homeless and seek shelter in a busy airport. While listening to this story, students will generate many questions. Quite a few of the questions will remain unanswered at the end of the text. Does this mean that the questions are not valid? Exactly the opposite! Books that leave students thinking, questioning, and wondering what happens next have initiated a dialogue between them and the author.

Generating questions helps students to fully engage in an intimate personal dialogue with the author. Each reader's questions are different, hence engagement with the text is a unique conversation for each reader. Two readers exposed to the same text may have completely different questions at any given point.

During Guided Listening, it is important for the teacher to acknowledge this variety of question types, and try to refrain from answering the students' questions. If you validate questions with a response such as "good question," or "interesting thought," rather than pointing out the answers, you help students search within the text to find their own answers. Although students may initially ask questions with answers that seem obvious to the teacher, they will gradually become more complex and meaningful as they become adept at formulating questions.

Synthesizing

Synthesizing is the process of combining the ideas presented in a text with one's own ideas to create something new and different. It is essentially the evolution of our ideas as we progress through a text. As we read, we are thinking of ideas, making sense of the words, and generating thoughts of our own.

When more information is added to our existing thoughts, we may broaden or alter our ideas. It is this self-reflection that defines synthesis. Not only are we thinking, but we are thinking about our thinking, reflecting on these thoughts and reshaping them to include new information. Confused yet? Debbie Miller (2002) uses an analogy that helps to visualize this process. Imagine dropping a pebble into a pond. The initial splash represents our initial ideas. The water begins to ripple in concentric circles, radiating out from that point, each ripple larger and more encompassing than the one before it. These ripples represent the new ideas stemming from, and building on, the initial idea. It's important that students be able to recognize their own ideas, but also have an awareness of how their ideas change and develop.

> **Prompts for Synthesizing**
>
> • Did you have an idea or thought that changed as we were reading?
> • How did your thinking evolve?
> • Did you change your mind about anything?
> • What did you add to your understanding?
> • What do you think the book is really about?
> • Do you feel differently now that you know more?
> • Why/how did your feelings change?

The picture book *The Stranger* by Chris Van Allsburg tells the story of a mysterious stranger arriving in the life of the Bailey family just as the summer is turning to fall. Mr. Bailey accidentally hits the stranger with his truck and the stranger seems to suffer some minor injuries—the worst is that he can not recall his identity. The family works together to try to help the stranger remember. Chris Van Allsburg brilliantly provides clues throughout the story that an attentive listener may be able to identify. Students need to carefully piece the clues together to determine the stranger's identity. After concluding this book, it is interesting to flip back through the story to find the clues that might have been overlooked the first time through. It's fantastic for students to experience the "ah-ha!" moment as they finally understand all of the strange events surrounding the stranger's presence.

One synthesizing activity is to have the students record jot notes as they are listening, and then retell the story to a partner.

Through Guided Listening, students can listen carefully for information that will contribute to their interpretation of the text.

Integrated Metacognition

In the Introduction to this book, we compared the complex processes of comprehension to the task of assembling a thousand-piece puzzle of a bowl of fruit. Usually, when we begin a complicated puzzle, we examine the picture on the box and use it as our guide throughout the process. In the same way, students need to have a clear image of what the effective use of comprehension strategies looks like. As teachers we, in fact, are the picture on the cover of their comprehension-puzzle boxes. They watch us closely for clues as to what to do, how to think, and how to use various strategies. We must make sure that the picture we present to students is clear and consistent.

As puzzle makers, after a thorough examination of the image on a puzzle box, we usually begin by sorting the puzzle pieces that will create the frame of the puzzle. In doing this, we build a scaffold into which all of the other pieces will fit. In the same way, presenting students with a framework on which to organize their ideas enables them to identify key ideas and record them.

Once we have completed the frame, we are set to begin to fill in the important features. In our fruit-bowl puzzle, we might select the red pieces to form the apple. We would know which pieces belong together because of their distinguishing features—in this case, color. As effective listeners and readers, each fruit represents a different comprehension strategy. We use different cues in the text for each strategy.

However, our bowl of fruit is not complete with an apple, or a banana, or even a bunch of grapes. The fruit-bowl puzzle requires that we complete each of these features in isolation; however, in order for the image to be clear, they must somehow fit together into a larger picture. As puzzle makers, we select pieces that fit together, and as readers we find important elements in the text that fit together to effectively use each of the strategies. Our puzzle is not complete until all of the fruits are linked together in a unified way; so, too, our understanding of text is not complete until we can integrate all of the metacognitive strategies into a larger picture. This integration of metacognitive strategies is the final step in the comprehension puzzle. Our goal is the big picture: students figuring out how to smoothly flow from inferring to asking questions, from making connections to determining important information, from visualizing to synthesizing, all the while understanding the text and thinking about their thinking.

4

The Mechanics of Guided Listening

"The teacher, if he is indeed wise, does not bid you to enter the house of wisdom but leads you to the threshold of your own mind."

—Kahlil Gilbran

The Procedure

Let's examine the sequence of a Guided Listening lesson that makes it so efficient.

> **Introduce:** Teacher begins by introducing the metacognitive strategy and reviewing its use.
>
> **Model:** Teacher completes read-aloud and students record and share their ideas.
>
> **Practice:** Students practice the skill with their independent reading and complete the lower portion of the Guided Listening worksheet.
>
> **Assess:** While students are independently reading, the teacher can review Guided Listening folders. Teachers can mark students' work from the previous day, record the marks, and conference if needed with any students.

1. Introduce the Strategy

Note that suggestions for instructions to give your class are in italics.

Before reading aloud, introduce students to the strategy they will be using during the read-aloud. This provides them with the background understanding of the strategy and how to use it. If a new strategy is being introduced, it may be necessary to spend a few minutes discussing the strategy with the students and ensuring that they understand what they will be required to do. For example,

> *Sometimes when I'm reading, I like to try to guess what is going to happen next. When I do this, I'm using some of the information in the book and my own thinking. I'm making a prediction. It's fun to try to guess what will happen, and then find out if the author had the same ideas as me or not. While you're listening, you need to try to use the information in the book and try to make a guess about what you think might happen next—Make a Prediction.*

When introducing a new strategy, always present the students with a general introduction of the strategy. Once the students become more familiar with each strategy, then a general reminder or review of the strategy and its definition will help students to focus their listening. When students have been introduced to a number of the different strategies, it is often beneficial to begin a Guided Listening lesson with a very quick overview of the different strategies: e.g., *What is one strategy that effective readers use? Inferencing—making conclusions about what we read; predicting—making a guess about what will happen;* etc.

2. Introduce the Organizer

Graphic organizers are visual representations of information. They provide students with a graphic way of collecting, organizing, and representing ideas.

A graphic organizer is an effective tool, a framework on which students can organize, represent, and share their ideas. In order for students to optimally utilize graphic organizers during Guided Listening, it is best that students have some familiarity with the graphic organizer before trying to apply it while learning a new strategy. Before the read-aloud, introduce students to the way they will record their thinking. This way, they will be certain of how to record their ideas.

It is not recommended that you introduce a new graphic organizer and a new comprehension strategy in the same lesson; e.g., *Let's use a Fishbone to record our inferences.* The purpose of introducing the organizer prior to the read-aloud is to scaffold the learning as much as possible, so the only thing the students need to think about is their thinking.

Establishing a purpose for listening is one of the key elements in Guided Listening. By informing the student of the tasks that they will be asked to complete as they are listening, you give them the opportunity to filter all of the information and pay specific attention to the key ideas that will be needed. When students are aware of the ways in which to organize the information they hear, it becomes easier for them to slot new information into the pre-established schema. Having a graphic organizer often assists students in critically selecting ideas.

Throughout this book a number of graphic organizers are used for a variety of purposes.

Venn Diagram

A Venn diagram (page 36) is the graphic organizer most commonly used to compare two or more concepts. Each circle represents a different idea. Students record ideas that are unique to each concept in the outer portions of the circles, and things they have in common in the centre portion. Venn diagrams are very useful for comparing characters, two books by the same author, or two or more books on a similar theme.

Idea Trail

An idea trail (page 37) helps students create a flow of connected ideas. In each box, students represent one idea—with a word, phrase, or illustration. Idea trails are useful for recording a number of ideas very quickly. It is interesting to discover the flow of thought that students had while listening.

The idea trail graphic organizer may be introduced to students using the following instructions:

Have you ever skipped down a path of stepping stones? Draw a simple idea trail (a series of boxes linked with arrows). *Sometimes our mind follows paths too, as we jump from one idea to another. The idea trail is a way of showing the path that your mind takes as you think about a series of ideas. Use each box to record a different idea, as your mind wanders from one idea to another.*

Web or Mind Map

A web or mind map (page 38) encourages students to find many different ideas that are connected to a central concept. Webs are useful for recording information about a character, describing setting, or providing evidence supporting a central theme. The central idea is placed in the centre of the web and connecting ideas are recorded in the surrounding spaces. Ideas can be represented with a word, phrase, or illustration. As students become more proficient at using webs or mind maps, they may begin to find additional connections between the ideas surrounding the central idea, or wish to further expand on one idea by adding more connections stemming from it. A web is a very versatile graphic organizer and encourages students to creatively expand it with their ideas.

Fishbone

A number of graphic organizers are provided for each of the strategies. The students enjoy the visual nature of the organizers and appreciate having a variety of ways to record their thinking. The more experience the students gain with the graphic organizers, the more creatively they will use them.

A fishbone (page 39) is used for representing a number of ideas and supporting details for each. Fishbones can have any number of branches, including any number of ideas. Students record a main idea on the top line of each branch, then add the supporting details under each main idea. Fishbones can be used for identifying the elements of narrative (setting, characters, plot), describing different characters, listing connections (text-to-text, text-to-self, text-to world), determining important ideas (and supporting details), etc.

The Fishbone graphic organizer may be introduced to students using the following instructions:

Draw a fishbone diagram on chart paper. *What does this graphic look like? This is called a fishbone, because it looks like the bones of a fish. The fishbone organizer we are going to use has _____ sections on it. Each section represents a different idea we will expand on. Each main idea is written on the top of a branch and the supporting details or evidence are added below each main idea.*

3. Model the Strategy

During the read-aloud, pause to model the use of the strategy. Teacher modelling provides students with insight into the thinking of readers. Encouraging students to share their thinking with a partner is also essential. Often students don't realize what they are thinking until they hear themselves speak. Verbalizing their thoughts makes their thinking tangible. Articulating ideas in conversation with their peers gives them the opportunity to express their thoughts, value and learn from the ideas of others, and seize thoughts that might slip away. Pausing while reading and allowing students to give voice to their ideas strengthens their metacognitive understanding.

4. Review the Text

After the read-aloud, encourage students to share their ideas with their peers. A minute is all that is necessary. In this way, students value and learn from the ideas of others and feel that they have had an opportunity to be heard themselves. If students are aware of this component of Guided Listening, they become more

After reading, encourage students to share their ideas with each other and with the large group. This is an excellent opportunity to correct any misunderstandings, or focus on creative, unique ideas. This process of reflecting on the text is invaluable! It helps students to understand how new ideas were formed and to strengthen their understanding of metacognitive strategies.

accountable for their learning, knowing that they will be required to share their thoughts at the end.

5. Review the Strategy

Before students begin to read independently, quickly refocus their attention on the comprehension strategy and the task they will complete on their own. This may be as simple as a summary sentence:

Remember, when we make predictions, we use clues in the story to help us guess what might happen next. While you're reading on your own, try to use the clues in the book to guess what you think might happen next.

6. Practice

Students read a book of their choosing to practice the strategy, using the same approach just modelled and shared. At first, it may be necessary to guide students while they are reading—they may be unfamiliar with pausing and recording their thinking. After a while, students become quite proficient are it.

7. Assess

The completed student worksheets are easy to assess, and give insight into students' thinking and learning. Assessments may be used for a variety of purposes, including determining areas for further instruction, grouping students according to areas of strength or need, and reporting student's progress.

Choosing Texts

Match the Text to the Task

"He that loves reading has everything within his reach."
—*William Godwin*

When introducing a new comprehension strategy to students, it is important to select a text that will make it easier for students to clearly apply the strategy being learned. Picture books work well when introducing a new strategy, as students are able to hear the text in its entirety and reflect on their thinking accordingly. The books listed here serve as great introductions for new strategies.

Making Inferences
Berger Barbara. *Grandfather Twilight*
Bunting, Eve. *Dandelion*
Bunting, Eve. *Fly Away Home*
dePaola, Tomie. *Oliver Button is a Sissy*
Mills, Lauren. *The Rag Coat*
Van Allsburg, Chris. *The Stranger*
Van Allsburg, Chris. *The Sweetest Fig*
Van Allsburg, Chris. *Bad Day at Riverbend*
Wyeth, Sharon Dennis. *Something Beautiful*
Yolen, Jane. *Mother Earth, Father Sky*
Zolotow, Charlotte. *If You Listen*

Making Predictions
Lottridge, Cecilia Barker. *The Name of the Tree*
Steig, William. *Brave Irene*
Steig, William. *Dr. DeSoto*
Watt, Melanie. *Scaredy Squirrel*

Determining Important Ideas
Turner, Ann. *Grasshopper Summer*
Van Allsburg, Chris. *The Widow's Broom*

Making Connections
Baillie, Allan. *Rebel*
Brinkloe, Julie. *Fireflies*
Bunting, Eve. *Going Home*
Chall, Marsha Wilson. *Up North at the Cabin*
Fox, Mem. *Koala Lou*
Henkes, Kevin. *Chrysanthemum*
Hoffman, Mary. *Amazing* Grace
Houston, Gloria. *My Great Aunt Arizona*
Levine, Ellen. *I Hate English*
Lobel, Arnold. *Frog and Toad are Friends*
Polacco, Patricia. *The Keeping Quilt*
Polacco, Patricia. *Some Birthday*
Polacco, Patricia. *Thank You Mr. Falker*
Rylant, Cynthia. *The Relatives Came*
Simon, James. *Dear Mr. Blueberry*
Steig, William. *Amos and Borris*
Viorst, Judith. *Alexander and the Terrible, Horrible, No Good, Very Bad Day*
Wells, Rosemary. *Hazel's Amazing Mother*

Visualizing
Baylor, Byrd. *I'm In Charge of Celebrations*
Brinkloe, Julie. *Fireflies*
Fletcher, Ralph. *Twilight Comes Twice*
Mazer, A. *The Salamander Room*
Wells, Rosemary. *Night Sounds, Morning Colors*
Yolen, Jane. *Color Me a Rhyme*

Asking Questions
Altman, Linda. *Amelia's Road*
Berger, Barbara. *Grandfather Twilight*
Bogart, Jo Ellen. *Jeremiah Learns to Read*
Bunting, Eve. *Fly Away Home*
Garland Sherry. *The Lotus Seed*
Van Allsburg, Chris. *The Stranger*

Synthesizing
Baylor, Byrd. *The Table Where Rich People Sit*
Bunting, Eve. *Smokey Night*
Lionni, Leo, *The Alphabet Tree*

Match the Task to the Text

As students become more familiar with the strategies, they can easily apply and continue to broaden their skills by listening to novels. When reading novels, it becomes important to match the task to the text. Selecting strategy activities that fit with the selected reading is important to consider.

If reading a series of books on a similar topic or by the same author, use strategy activities that naturally encourage students to see connections between them. Students should also be encouraged to draw on their knowledge from other subject areas—integrating their learning.

Understanding a Variety of Media Forms

Life in the 21st century requires media literacy. It is important that students develop strong critical thinking skills in order to understand and effectively interpret a variety of media forms.

According to the Centre for Media Literacy (Share, Jolls and Thoman; 2005), there are five key questions that students should consider when examining various media forms:

1. Who created the message?
2. What creative techniques are effectively used in the media?
3. How do different people interpret the message?
4. What values are embedded in the message?
5. Why is the message being sent?

Using these five key questions as a guide, let's examine the implications they have when presenting a variety of media forms for use with Guided Listening.

Key Question	Using Different Media Forms with Guided Listening
1. Who created the message? While examining media forms, students should keep in mind that all media is constructed. Guiding students to examine the choices that went into the construction of the message will give them insight into what was included and excluded to make the message effective.	Comparing a movie to the book it was based on provides a perfect opportunity for students to critically evaluate the choices made while creating the movie. Students will find similarities and differences between the two, and form an opinion as to the interpretive changes that were made to the original text.
2. What creative techniques are effectively used in the media? As students become more analytical of various media forms, they will be able to identify techniques used to convey the message of the media. These include body language, background music, lighting, tone of voice, creative movement, etc.	Students can note creative techniques (lighting, sound, music, body language, tone of voice, etc.) and think about how these strategies helped them to visualize or to further deepen their understanding or interpretation of the media.

Key Question	Using Different Media Forms with Guided Listening
3. How do different people interpret the message? The way we understand messages depends heavily on our personal background. No two people see the same movie or hear the same song in the same way. Each person uses a unique set of experiences to interpret the media.	Encourage students to form connections between their previous experiences and media presentations. Each student will bring a different interpretation to a media presentation, simply because of the different perspectives with which they view it. It is interesting for students to consider the target audience for a given media message.
4. What values are embedded in the message? The choices that are made while constructing a media message often reflect values, points of view, or stereotypes. Some of these include the age, gender, and race of people portrayed, the setting, and vocabulary used.	Encouraging students to think about the point of view or to infer the main idea of the message will require them to become more aware of the hidden features. Discussing with students the decision to include or exclude certain things and to question the values presented will help them develop the critical analysis skills necessary in the diverse world in which we live.
5. Why is the message being sent? We need to examine the motive or purpose for the media message, beyond the obvious purposes of entertaining, informing, and persuading. Most media messages involve elements of commercialism.	Critically looking at magazines or newspapers to note the placement, size, and general style of advertisements gives insight into the targeted audience.

Adapted from Share, J. Jolls, T. and Thoman, E. (2005).

Graphic Organizer:
Venn Diagrams

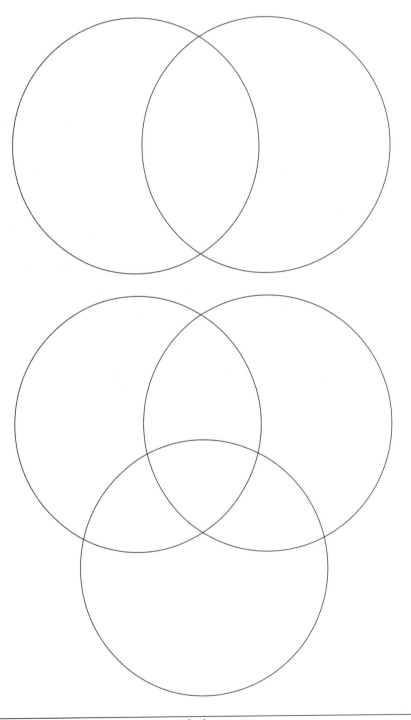

Graphic Organizer:
Idea Trail

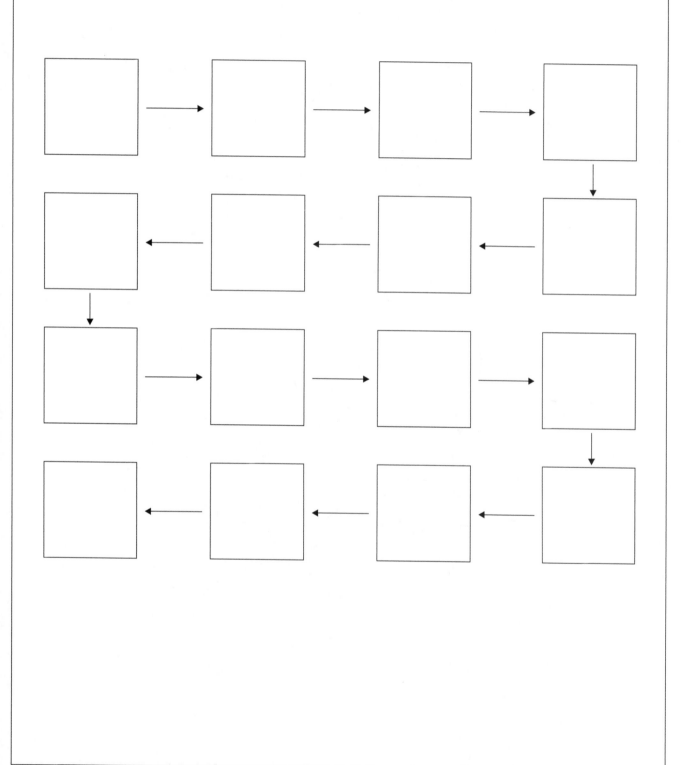

Graphic Organizer:
Webs or Mind Maps

Graphic Organizer: Fishbones

5

Making Inferences and Predictions

"Life does not consist mainly, or even largely, of facts and happenings. It consists mainly of the storm of thoughts that are forever blowing through one's mind."

—*Mark Twain*

Making Inferences

Introduce Making Inferences

"Inferring is giving a logical guess based on facts or evidence presented using prior knowledge to help the reader understand the deeper meaning of a text."
—etools4education

When introducing the strategy of Making Inferences, you may need to spend a few minutes discussing the strategy with the students so they have a good understanding of what they will need to do. Subsequent lessons will require varying amounts of introduction, until students become proficient with the concept of Making Inferences. They will need to hear the information from the introduction many times, but in different ways. The introduction and lessons below are meant to serve as a guide for discussions, not instructions to be quoted verbatim.

The teacher may introduce Making Inferences with an introduction like the following:

Before beginning to read aloud, outline the expectations for the students.

Effective readers use the information in the text to make conclusions about what they are reading. Sometimes an author might be trying to teach us an important lesson, or we might use clues in a story to figure out how a character feels. When we do this, we are making inferences. There are many different types of inferences we can make, and different people might make different inferences from the same story. We might not find out if out inference is "correct" or not—because the author does not usually tell us. It is a conclusion that we come to from the clues in the text.

Identifying Main Idea/Theme

Use worksheet *Making Inferences: Identifying Main Idea/Theme* on page 45.

Students listen to the text and try to summarize the main idea or theme of the book. Encourage students to think of the important lesson the author wanted them to learn from the text. Provide students with examples: *Even though you're small, you can do big things,* or *All people need to be treated with respect.* During and after reading, pause and encourage students to share their ideas with a partner or the large group.

MAKING INFERENCES

Making conclusions and predictions; evaluating, judging and reflecting on my reading.

Today I <u>**listened to**</u> the book: Thank you Mr. Falker

While I was listening, I figured out that the main idea (theme) the author wanted us to learn from this book is...

If you need help with something you should keep trying and never give up.

Today I <u>**read**</u> the book: James and the Giant Peach

While I was reading, I figured out that the main idea (theme) the author wanted me to learn from the book is...

Keep trying and reach your goal even when problems are in your way.

Inferring a Character's Feelings

Use worksheet *Making Inferences: Inferring a Character's Feelings* on page 46.

Students listen to the story and use the clues in the text to determine the feelings of the character. While reading, place emphasis on phrases that describe body language, tone of voice, or surrounding circumstances.

When we are reading we need to look for clues that tell us how the characters are feeling. For example, an author might say, "Sara's heart raced and the hair on the back of her neck stood up. She held her breath and could hear her heart pounding in her chest." How would you describe how Sara is feeling, and which clues helped you to figure that out? As you are listening, try to find clues about how the characters are feeling. Remember to include the evidence from the text that helped you.

Pause during and after reading to allow time for students to share their thinking with a partner or with the large group.

Evaluating

Use worksheets *Making Inferences: Evaluating Positively* on page 47 and *Making Inferences: Evaluating Negatively* on page 48.

Students listen to the text and evaluate it critically. Encourage students to think of things they liked or disliked while listening: something a character does, something that happens, or even the way the author chooses to end the story. Pause during reading to allow time for students to share their thinking with a partner. After reading, encourage students to share their evaluations with partners or the large group. They may choose to include their own ideas in the evaluation: e.g. "I didn't like the way the main character spoke to his mother…" "If I were the author, I would have said…"

Point of View

Use worksheets *Making Inferences: Point of View* on page 49 and *Making Inferences: Choosing a Point of View* on page 50.

Students listen to the book and evaluate the perspective from which it is being told. When we hear a story, the "version" we get depends greatly on who is telling it. If the same story were told by someone else, we might hear a completely different point of view. As students listen to the book, they should think about who is telling the story. Encourage students to think about the other characters and consider alternate points of view. After reading, encourage students to share their thinking with a partner or with the large group.

MAKING INFERENCES

Making conclusions and predictions; evaluating, judging and reflecting on my reading.

Today I **listened to** the book: Something Beautiful

If you could hear this story from another point of view, whose story would you like to hear? Why?

If I could hear this story, "Something Beautiful" from another point of view I would want to hear the homeless person's story. This is because I would want to hear how the homeless person survives on the street with no money, food, shelter, water, etc. I would also want to hear how the person looks at life, if she thinks thinks life is unfair and if she has something beautiful in her life.

Today I **read** the book: Inkheart

If you could hear this story from another point of view, whose story would you like to hear? Why?

If I could hear this story, "Inkheart" from another point of view I would want to hear a mysterious character's story named Dustfinger. This is because Dustfinger has a hard life, he does not belong in this world and he can not get used to it. I would want to hear Dustfinger's hardships and how he survives in this fast flowing world. I would also want to hear what Dustfinger thinks of our world and what he misses in his other world.

In Role

Use worksheet *Making Inferences: In Role* on page 51.

Students listen to the story and consider the decisions and actions of one of the characters. They are to use their own ideas and experiences to think about what they may have done if they were in a similar situation.

As we listen to stories, we often have ideas that seem different from those of the characters. Have you ever wanted to shout at the television, or help a character through a challenge? When we put ourselves in the character's place, we are using our own experiences and knowledge to help us make inferences. As you are listening, think of what you would have done if you were the main character.

Pausing at critical points in the story and encouraging students to share their thinking with a partner will help students to formulate their ideas. After reading, students should again share their thinking with a partner.

MAKING INFERENCES

Making conclusions and predictions; evaluating, judging and reflecting on my reading.

Today I <u>**listened to**</u> the book: Oliver Button is a Sissy

If I were the main character...

I would feel sad because I wouldn't like to be called sissy. I would have felt happy because I would love to be called a star

Today I <u>**read**</u> the book: Why Can't I Fly

If I were the main character...

I would feel sad and mad if I couldn't fly in the air. I would have felt happy if I could fly in the fresh air.

Valuing Ideas of Others

Use worksheet *Making Inferences: Valuing Ideas of Others* on page 52.

Students listen to the story and the ideas of their peers. Instructions like the following may help clarify the directions for the students:

We each have fantastic ideas on our own, but sometimes it is important to listen to the ideas of others. While you are listening, we will pause to share our inferences at various points in the story. You need to listen to the inferences made by your classmates and record one of them. Once you have recorded someone else's inference, tell whether you agree with it or not. Justify your thinking.

It is important to pause at various points while reading and encourage students to share their inferences with partners or the large group. After reading, allow a few minutes for students to share the ideas they recorded with partners or the large group.

Introduce Independent Reading

Remind students of the strategy Making Inferences. Instructions like the following may be helpful:

> *When you begin to read on your own, think about the way we made inferences together. Remember that when we make inferences, we are using the clues in the story to help us come to conclusions. Try to use the clues in your independent reading book to make similar inferences.*

Students should read an independent reading book of their choice and practice the skill that was the focus for instruction.

Name: _____ Date: _____

Making Inferences
Identifying Main Idea/Theme

Evaluating, judging, and reflecting on my listening and reading

Today I **listened to** the book: _____

While I was listening, I figured out that the main idea (theme) the author wanted us to learn from this book is...

_____

_____

_____

_____

Today I **read** the book:_____

While I was reading, I figured out that the main idea (theme) the author wanted me to learn from the book is...

_____

_____

_____

_____

Name: _____ Date: _____

Making Inferences
Inferring a Character's Feelings

Evaluating, judging, and reflecting on my listening and reading

Today I **listened to** the book: _____

If I had to guess how the main character was feeling at the end, I think...

_____

_____

_____

_____

_____

Today I **read** the book:_____

While I was reading, I thought that the main character was feeling _____ because...

_____

_____

_____

_____

_____

Name: _____ Date: _____

Making Inferences
Evaluating Positively

Evaluating, judging, and reflecting on my listening and reading

Today I **listened to** the book: _____

I really liked how...

_____

_____

_____

_____

_____

Today I **read** the book: _____

I really liked how...

_____

_____

_____

_____

_____

Name: _____ Date: _____

Making Inferences
Evaluating Negatively

Evaluating, judging, and reflecting on my listening and reading

Today I **listened to** the book: _____

What I didn't like was...

_____

_____

_____

_____

_____

Today I **read** the book: _____

What I didn't like was...

_____

_____

_____

_____

_____

Name: _____ Date: _____

Making Inferences
Point of View

Evaluating, judging, and reflecting on my listening and reading

Today I **listened to** the book: _____

How would the story have been different if one of the other characters were telling it?

_____

_____

_____

_____

_____

Today I **read** the book: _____

How would the story have been different if one of the other characters were telling it?

_____

_____

_____

_____

_____

Name: _____ Date: _____

Making Inferences
Choosing a Point of View

Evaluating, judging, and reflecting on my listening and reading

Today I **listened to** the book: _____

If you could hear this story from another point of view, whose story would you like to hear? Why?

_____

_____

_____

_____

_____

Today I **read** the book: _____

If you could read this story from another point of view, whose story would you like to read? Why?

_____

_____

_____

_____

_____

Name: _____ Date: _____

Making Inferences
In Role

Evaluating, judging, and reflecting on my listening and reading

Today I **listened to** the book:_____

If I were the main character...

_____

_____

_____

_____

_____

Today I **read** the book:_____

If I were the main character...

_____

_____

_____

_____

_____

Name: _____ Date: _____

Making Inferences
Valuing Ideas of Others

Evaluating, judging, and reflecting on my listening and reading

Today I **listened to** the book:_____

My classmates made the following inferences (conclusions, predictions, evaluations, reflections) while we read the story:

_____

_____

_____

_____

_____

Today I **read** the book:_____

While I was reading, I made the following inferences:

_____

_____

_____

_____

_____

Making Predictions

"Predicting is using the text to guess what will happen next. Then the reader confirms or rejects their prediction as they read."
—etools4education

Introduce Making Predictions

Begin with an introduction to the strategy of Making Predictions. As students become more comfortable with the strategy, subsequent lessons will require varying amounts of introduction. Students' understanding of Making Predictions will be strengthened if they hear the same ideas in a variety of ways.

Instructions like the following may be used as a general introduction to Making Predictions:

Before beginning to read aloud, outline the expectations for the students.

Effective readers use the information in the text to make predictions about what they are reading. Sometimes, the author gives us clues about what is going to happen. We need to use clues in the story and our own ideas to take a guess about what we think will happen next. A prediction is different than an inference, because we will usually find out if our prediction was right or not.

Supporting Evidence

Use worksheet *Making Predictions: Finding Clues* on page 56 and *Making Predictions: Supporting Evidence* on page 57.

Students listen to the text and try to identify clues that will help them formulate predictions. While reading, pause at a critical point in the story and provide an opportunity for students to share their predictions. When students record their predictions, they should include the clues from the story that helped them to make their predictions. After reading, encourage students to share their thinking with partners.

MAKING PREDICTIONS

Making a guess about what might happen next.

Today I **listened to** the book: Where are you going Manyoni?

While I was listening, I predicted:
I think she will go into the grassland.

I thought this would happen because:
I think this would happen because she gets closer to trees and animals.

Today I **read** the book: Sea Monster Scare

While I was reading, I predicted:
that the seamonster will come.

I thought this would happen because:
everybody left and there was something red sticking out of the water.

MAKING PREDICTIONS

Making a guess about what might happen next.

Today I **listened to** the book: The Empty Pot

While I was listening, I predicted:

While I was listening I predicted that the child that has the most beautiful flower still won't be the next emperor because the emperor won't be pleased with the child. I think he won't be pleased with him/her because the child cheated by using another seed that grows to be better and beautiful and the emperor was aware of this because he gave them bad seeds intentionally.

I was sure this would happen because the author said:

I was sure this would happen because I made a text-to-text connection with another story that had a similar beginning and so I combined my prior knowledge with some new ideas to create a new idea for my conclusion.

Today I **read** the book: The City of Ember

While I was reading, I predicted:

While I was reading I predicted that Lina's plan involved taking her younger sister, Poppy from their kind guardian named Mrs. Murdo because she'd wanted to take Poppy along on her journey with Doon.

I found the following sentence from the book to support my idea:

I found the sentence from the book which said, "Once the lights go back on Lina would put her plan into action." This sentence stated that she had a plan and previously she didn't want to leave Poppy and it was very difficult for her to leave without Poppy so she continued on her way with Doon. Then her and Doon got seaperated and she had the perfect oppertunity to get her sister and bring her to the city which needed to be discovered and once it was, their dying city that was falling apart would be saved and Doon and Lina were seceretly going to make this discovery and then share it with the rest of their city.

Evaluating Predictions

Use worksheet *Making Predictions: Evaluating Predictions* on page 58.

Students listen to the story, and use the clues in the story and their own ideas to make a prediction about what they think might happen next. Pausing at a pivotal point provides students an opportunity to think about a reasonable prediction and record their ideas. After students have recorded their predictions, continue reading the story. After reading, students should reflect on the prediction they recorded and determine if it was correct or not. If their prediction was not correct, they should consider the ways in which the author's ideas were different from theirs. After reading, encourage students to share their thinking with a partner or the large group.

Valuing Ideas of Others

Use worksheet *Making Predictions: Valuing Ideas of Others* on page 59.

Students listen to the ideas in the book and the ideas of their peers. While reading, pause at critical moments and encourage students to share their predictions. As students are listening to the predictions of their peers, they should record one of the predictions made by a classmate. Once they have recorded a prediction, they should record whether or not they agree with the prediction and justify their thinking, using evidence from the text or their own thinking.

Introduce Independent Reading Activity

Review the strategy Making Predictions. When students begin to read on their own, they should think about the way in which predictions were made together. Remind students that they should use clues in the story and their own ideas to try to guess what will happen next. Encourage students to record their ideas and try to provide reasons (proof) from the book that helped them make their predictions.

Name: _____ Date: _____

Making Predictions
Finding Clues

Making a guess about what might happen next

Today I **listened to** the book: _____

While I was listening, I predicted...

_____

_____

I thought this would happen because

_____

_____

_____

_____

Today I **read** the book: _____

While I was reading, I predicted...

_____

_____

I thought this would happen because

_____

_____

_____

_____

Name: _____ Date: _____

Making Predictions
Supporting Evidence

Making a guess about what might happen next

Today I **listened to** the book: _____

While I was listening, I predicted...

_____

_____

I was sure this would happen because the author said

_____

_____

_____

Today I **read** the book: _____

While I was reading, I predicted...

_____

_____

_____

I found the following sentence from the book to support my idea:

_____

_____

_____

Name: _____ Date: _____

Making Predictions
Evaluating Predictions

Making a guess about what might happen next

Today I **listened to** the book: _____

While I was listening, I predicted...

_____

_____

After listening, I found out

_____

_____

_____

_____

Today I **read** the book: _____

While I was reading, I predicted...

_____

_____

After reading, I found out

_____

_____

_____

_____

Name: _____ Date: _____

Making Predictions
Valuing Ideas of Others

Making a guess about what might happen next

Today I **listened to** the book: _____

My classmate made this prediction:

_____

_____

I agree/disagree with this prediction because

_____

_____

_____

_____

Today I **read** the book: _____

While I was reading, I predicted...

_____

_____

After reading, I found out

_____

_____

_____

_____

6

Determining Important Ideas

"Unless you try to do something beyond what you have already mastered, you will never grow."

—*Ralph Waldo Emerson*

Introduce Determining Important Ideas

The teacher may begin with an introduction similar to the following:

When we use the strategy Determining Important Ideas, we are thinking critically about the text and trying to figure out what information is the most important. Some ideas in a book tell us critical facts that contribute to the book, while some other ideas are there to make the book more interesting or fun to read. While listening, try to think of which ideas you feel are the most important and record those on your sheet.

Before beginning to read aloud, outline the expectations for the students.

Identifying Key Concepts

Students listen critically and identify ideas that they think are important. They should record these ideas on the sheet provided. It may be helpful to pause during reading and encourage students to share their thinking with partners or with the large group. Encourage students to continue to add to their ideas as new information is revealed. They may wish to revisit ideas that they initially thought were important, and revise or change them.

Use worksheets *Determining Important Ideas: Identifying Important Concepts* on page 63 ; *Using a Web* on page 64; *Using an Idea Trail* on page 65; *Using a Fishbone* on page 66.

If using a graphic organizer:
- A review of how to use this organizer may be needed.
- On certain graphic organizers (web and idea trail) students may be encouraged to record their ideas using words, phrases, sentences, or illustrations.

Summarizing

Use worksheet *Determining Important Ideas: Summarizing* on page 67.

Students listen carefully to the text and summarize the main idea. Informing students of this task prior to reading will help them to break the text into its key elements. It may be helpful to have students summarize the text with a partner before beginning to write.

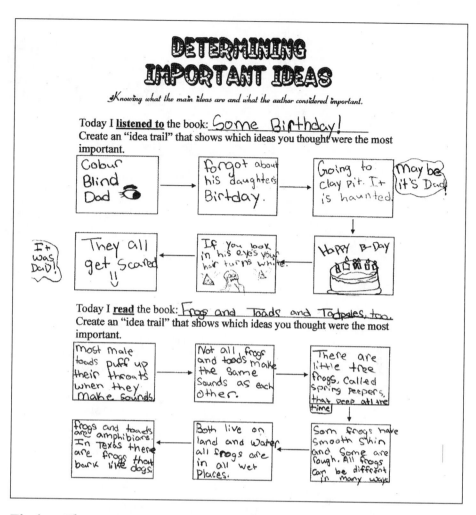

Fiction Elements

Use worksheet *Determining Important Ideas: Fiction Elements* on page 68.

Students listen carefully in order to identify the three elements of a fictional text: setting, characters, theme/main idea. They may wish to record their ideas using words, sentences, phrases, or illustrations. It may be challenging, at first, for students to identify the theme or main idea of a story. This may be an area for discussion prior to read-aloud, and an area for modelling during and after the read-aloud.

Sequencing

Use worksheet *Determining Important Ideas: Sequencing* on page 69.

Students listen carefully in order to identify three important events or ideas that happen sequentially in the text. Students will have to listen critically in order to select the thee most important ideas. Encourage students to share their thoughts with partners or with the whole class. After reading, asking students to share which three ideas they recorded and justify their choice (why they thought it was an important idea) can lead to a valuable discussion.

DETERMINING IMPORTANT IDEAS

Knowing what the main ideas are and what the author considered important.

Today I **listened to** the book: Koala Lou

In this story...

First — Everyone loved Koala Lou and her mother told her that she loved her all the time.

Then — Koala lou's mom stopped telling her she loved her so she decided to compete in the olympics.

Finally — Koala Lou came in second and her mom finaly said she loved her and she always will.

Today I **read** the book: Puss-in-boots

In this story...

First — There was a miller when he died he gave everuthing to his three sons.

Then — The youngest son got a cat it was a magic cat he caube talk.

Finally — The youngest son got married to the princess.

Identifying Main Idea

Use worksheet *Determining Important Ideas: Identifying Main Idea* on page 70.

Students listen carefully in order to identify one main idea from the text. Students may choose to record a new fact that they have learned, some important information about one of the characters in the story, a new twist in the plot, or the moral (lesson) of the story. It may be helpful for students to share their thinking with partners and provide support for their ideas after reading.

Critical Reflection

Use worksheet *Determining Important Ideas: Critical Reflection* on page 71.

Students listen for key concepts. As they hear something they think is an important idea, they record their thinking in the first box. They may choose to record their ideas with pictures, words, phrases, etc. As they continue to listen, they may have new ideas to add, or may decide that some ideas are no longer relevant; they can record this in the second box. After reading, they may wish to reflect on the ideas that they initially thought were important. Again, sharing their thinking with partners or the large group may be beneficial.

Introduce Independent Reading Activity

Review the strategy of Determining Important Ideas. Encourage students to focus their attention on identifying key ideas and recording these while reading independently. Review the activity that students will complete while reading and the way in which they are to record their responses.

Name: _____ Date: _____

Determining Important Ideas
Identifying Important Concepts

Figuring out the main ideas and key concepts

Today I **listened to** the book: _____

The most important ideas are:

- _____
- _____
- _____
- _____

Today I **read** the book: _____

The most important ideas are:

- _____
- _____
- _____
- _____

Name: _____   Date: _____

Determining Important Ideas
Using a Web

Figuring out the main ideas and key concepts

Today I **listened to** the book: _____

Create a web of the ideas you think are important:

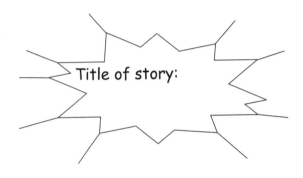

Title of story:

Today I **read** the book: _____

Create a web of the ideas you think are important:

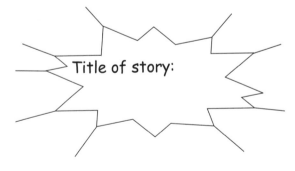

Title of story:

Name: _____ Date: _____

Determining Important Ideas
Using an Idea Trail

Figuring out the main ideas and key concepts

Today I **listened to** the book: _____

Create an idea trail that shows which ideas you thought were the most important.

```
┌─────────┐      ┌─────────┐      ┌─────────┐
│         │ ──→  │         │ ──→  │         │
│         │      │         │      │         │
└─────────┘      └─────────┘      └────┬────┘
                                       │
                                       ↓
┌─────────┐      ┌─────────┐      ┌─────────┐
│         │ ←──  │         │ ←──  │         │
│         │      │         │      │         │
└─────────┘      └─────────┘      └─────────┘
```

Today I **read** the book: _____

Create an idea trail that shows which ideas you thought were the most important.

```
┌─────────┐      ┌─────────┐      ┌─────────┐
│         │ ──→  │         │ ──→  │         │
│         │      │         │      │         │
└─────────┘      └─────────┘      └────┬────┘
                                       │
                                       ↓
┌─────────┐      ┌─────────┐      ┌─────────┐
│         │ ←──  │         │ ←──  │         │
│         │      │         │      │         │
└─────────┘      └─────────┘      └─────────┘
```

Determining Important Ideas Using a Fishbone

Figuring out the main ideas and key concepts

Name: _____   Date: _____

Today I **listened to** the book: _____

Using the fishbone diagram, identify three important ideas. Under each idea, provide the evidence from the book that made you think that this idea was important.

Title of story:

Today I **read** the book: _____

Using the fishbone diagram, identify three important ideas. Under each idea, provide the evidence from the book that made you think that this idea was important.

Title of story:

Name: _____ Date: _____

Determining Important Ideas
Summarizing

Figuring out the main ideas and key concepts

Today I **listened to** the book: _____

The book was about…

_____

_____

_____

_____

_____

_____

Today I **read** the book: _____

The book was about…

_____

_____

_____

_____

_____

_____

Name: _____ Date: _____

Determining Important Ideas
Fiction Elements

Figuring out the main ideas and key concepts

Today I **listened to** the book: _____

While I was listening, I thought the following ideas about the setting, characters, and theme were important.

Setting	Characters	Theme

Today I **read** the book: _____

While I was reading, I thought the following ideas about the setting, characters, and theme were important.

Setting	Characters	Theme

Name: _____ Date: _____

Determining Important Ideas
Sequencing

Figuring out the main ideas and key concepts

Today I **listened to** the book: _____

In this book:...

First _____

_____

Then _____

_____

Finally _____

_____

Today I **read** the book:_____

In this book:...

First _____

_____

Then _____

_____

Finally _____

_____

Name: _____ Date: _____

Determining Important Ideas
Identifying Main Idea

Figuring out the main ideas and key concepts

Today I **listened to** the book: _____

Something I learned was...

_____

_____

_____

_____

_____

_____

Today I **read** the book: _____

Something I learned was...

_____

_____

_____

_____

_____

Name: _____ Date: _____

Determining Important Ideas
Critical Reflection

Figuring out the main ideas and key concepts

Today I **listened to** the book: _____

When I first started listening, I thought it was important that	After listening, I **now** think it is important that

Today I **read** the book: _____

When I first started reading, I thought it was important that	After reading, I **now** think it is important that

7

Making Connections

"We must not, in trying to think about how we can make a big difference, ignore the small daily differences we can make which, over time, add up to big differences that we often cannot foresee."

—*Marian Wright Edelman*

Introduce Making Connections

Helping students to undertand the three types of connections will help them to identify the connections that they are able to make:

Effective readers make connections to the story as they are reading. This means that they think about what they already know and connect it to the ideas they find in the story. Sometimes we think about how the story connects to our own lives (maybe we've had a similar experience, or know someone like one of the characters in the story). These connections are called Text-to-Self connections.

Another type of connection we may make is called Text-to-Text. As we read books, we sometimes think of ways they are similar to other books we have read.

Finally, as critical readers, we evaluate the information from the text with things we know about the world. We use our knowledge of the world to have a deeper understanding of the text. This type of connection is called a Text-to-World connection.

When we make connections, we need to think of two things—one from the story we are reading, and the other from our personal experiences—and describe the link between these two things. It is not enough to say that a character is like your mother; you must say why. The why *is the important part. The* why *is the link that connects the two independent ideas.*

Before beginning to read aloud, outline the expectations for the students.

Encourage students to record connections from throughout the reading selection, not only the beginning. Also, remind students of the importance of including the link between the two ideas.

General Connections

Use worksheets *Making Connections: General Connections* on page 77; *Visual Connections* on page 78; and *Text Connections* on page 79.

Students listen to the text and record ideas that they are reminded of. They may think of another book, another person or character, a personal experience, or something they may have encountered in other media (e.g., TV, movie, video game). Encourage students to record the idea, as well as how it is connected to the text being read aloud: e.g., "This story made me think of my great aunt Matilda because she makes pancakes, just like the Grandma in the story." The reason for the connection is just as important as the connection itself. After reading, it is helpful to encourage students to share their connections with a partner.

MAKING CONNECTIONS

Using what I know to help me understand the text.

Today I **listened to** the book: LOSER

This book makes me think of....

* That I am in grade five and didn't have a best until my two friends agreed to be my best friend!
* Another connection is that I made Snickerdoodles, Zinkoff made them too!

Today I **read** the book: Sisterhood of the Traveling Pants

This book makes me think of...

* When I go away on vacation, and my friends are not with me.
* Tibby reminds me of when I use the video tape to make a movie/documentary.

MAKING CONNECTIONS

Using what I know to help me understand the text.

Today I **listened to** the book: Franklin is Bossy

The part of the story where... Franklin was bossy to bear.

Reminds me of... When I was bossy to my friend.

Today I **read** the book: My home is just right for me

The part of the story where... the dog was chasing the cat

Reminds me of... When I was scared of a big black dog, and I was crying too.

Character Connections in Fiction

Students listen to the text, focusing their attention on the characters in the story. For these activities, it is important to choose texts that students will connect with easily. Selecting books in which the characters are a similar age or in a similar situation as the students will make it easer for them to initially form connections. As students gain more experience, they will begin to make broader connections and think of ways to relate to characters in a text. Pausing during reading for

Use worksheets *Making Connections: Character Connections in Fiction* on page 80; *Character Connections Using Venn Diagrams* on page 81; and *Character Connections Using a Fishbone* on page 82.

brief moments of discussion (in a large group or with a partner) may help to spark some connections for students who may be struggling with the activity. After reading, it is useful for students to share their ideas with a partner.

If using a graphic organizer:
- It may be necessary to review how to effectively use the tool prior to beginning the lesson.
- When using the Venn diagram, students may record their ideas using words, phrases, or illustrations.

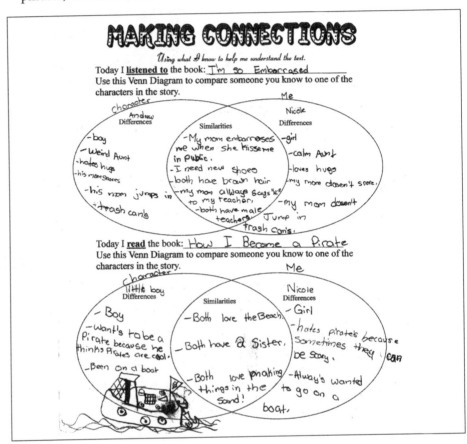

Text-to-Text Connections

Use worksheets *Making Connections: Connections to Another Book* on page 83; *Connections to Television* on page 84; *Text-to-Text Connections* on page 85.

Students listen to the text and try to identify connections to other texts. Initially this activity works best with texts for which connections are easily made; for example, a variety texts on a similar subject or by the same author, or texts that take place in the same time period (e.g., medieval Europe or the future). To start, it may be necessary to create obvious opportunities for students to make text-to-text connections, but they will rapidly master this skill and begin to make connections independently and creatively. If students are struggling to make connections, it can be helpful to pause briefly when reading aloud and encourage students to share their thinking with their partners. After reading it is always beneficial for students to share their connections with partners or the large group.

If using the Venn diagram, it may be necessary to review how to effectively use this tool (using words, phrases, or illustrations) prior to beginning the lesson.

Personal Experiences

Using worksheet *Making Connections: Text-to-Self Connections* on page 86.

Students listen to the text and record a personal experience that connects them to the text. The use of a Venn diagram may need to be reviewed prior to beginning the lesson. Students may record their ideas with pictures, words, or phrases. When recording their ideas, it is important for students to think of ways their experience is similar to and different from that in the text. A time for sharing during or after reading would be beneficial.

Three Types of Connections

Using worksheets *Making Connections: Using a Web* on page 87; *Using an Idea Trail* on page 88; and *Three Types of Connections* on page 89.

Students listen to the text and record connections they have to the text. These activities should be used once students have a general understanding of how to make connections and have spent some time making a variety of types of connections. Before reading aloud, review with students the nature of each type of connection (text-to-text, text-to-self, and text-to-world). Pausing during reading and reflecting after reading will help students to see their connections more clearly and to appreciate the connections made by their peers.

If using a graphic organizer:

- The use of the graphic organizer may need to be reviewed prior to the lesson.
- When using the web or Venn diagram, students may choose to record their thinking with words, phrases, or illustrations.

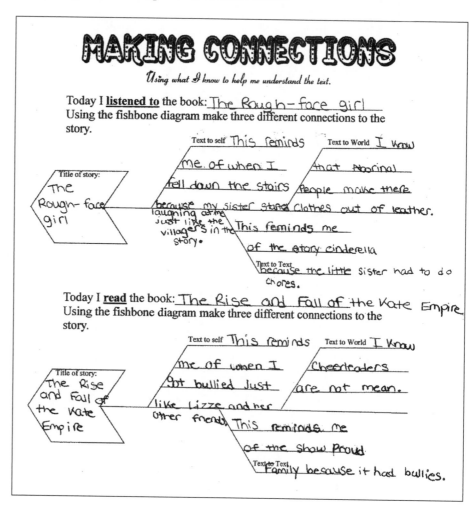

Valuing Ideas of Others

Using worksheet *Making Connections: Valuing Ideas of Others* on page 90.

Students listen to the text and the connections made by their peers. During reading, pause frequently and encourage students to share their connections with partners or with the large group. As students listen to the ideas of their classmates, they are to record connections that they think are interesting. It is important for students to recognize, appreciate, and value the ideas of others. This collaborative approach to learning teaches students that they need to listen to each other as well as to the teacher.

Introduce Independent Reading Activity

Review the strategy of Making Connections. Remind students that as they are reading on their own they should try to think about how the ideas in the story connect with their own ideas. Encourage students to focus on all three types of connections: Text-to-Text (other books with similar ideas, themes, or characters), Text-to-Self (personal experiences that are similar to those in the book), and Text-to-World (things they know about the world and how they help a reader understand the book). It is very important that students try to think of how and why their ideas are connected to the ones in the book.

Name: _____ Date: _____

Making Connections
General Connections

Using my own experiences to help me understand the text

Today I **listened to** the book: _____

This book makes me think of...

_____

_____

_____

_____

_____

_____

Today I **read** the book: _____

This book makes me think of...

_____

_____

_____

_____

_____

_____

Name: _____   Date: _____

Making Connections
Visual Connections

Using my own experiences to help me understand the text

Today I **listened to** the book: _____

The picture in the book where_____

_____

Reminds me of _____

_____

_____

_____

_____

Today I **read** the book:_____

The picture in the book where_____

_____

Reminds me of _____

_____

_____

_____

_____

Name: _____ Date: _____

Making Connections
Text Connections

Using my own experiences to help me understand the text

Today I **listened to** the book: _____

The part of the story where _____

_____

Reminds me of _____

_____

_____

_____

_____

Today I **read** the book: _____

The part of the story where _____

_____

Reminds me of _____

_____

_____

_____

_____

Name: _____ Date: _____

Making Connections
Character Connections in Fiction

Using my own experiences to help me understand the text

Today I **listened to** the book: _____

One character in this book reminds me of someone I know:

_____

_____

_____

_____

_____

_____

_____

Today I **read** the book: _____

One character in this book reminds me of someone I know:

_____

_____

_____

_____

_____

_____

Name: _____ Date: _____

Making Connections
Character Connections Using Venn Diagrams

Using my own experiences to help me understand the text

Today I **listened to** the book: _____

Use the Venn diagram to compare someone you know to one of the characters in the story.

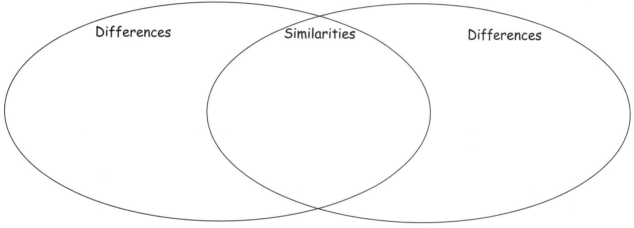

Today I **read** the book: _____

Use the Venn diagram to compare someone you know to one of the characters in the story.

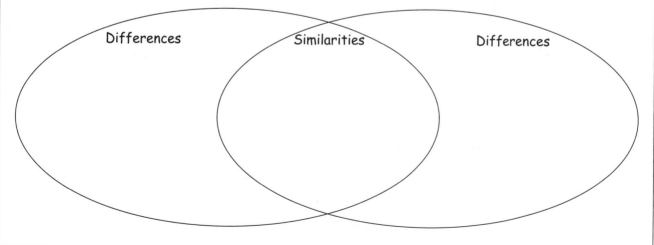

Name: _____ Date: _____

Making Connections
Character Connections Using a Fishbone

Using my own experiences to help me understand the text

Today I **listened to** the book: _____

Using the fishbone diagram, list ways you can connect to four of the characters in the story.

Character: _____   Character: _____

Title of story: _____

Character: _____   Character: _____

Today I **read** the book: _____

Using the fishbone diagram, list ways you can connect to four of the characters in the story.

Character: _____   Character: _____

Title of story: _____

Character: _____   Character: _____

Name: _____ Date: _____

Making Connections
Connections to Another Book

Using my own experiences to help me understand the text

Today I **listened to** the book: _____

This book reminded me of another book I've read:

_____

_____

_____

_____

_____

_____

Today I **read** the book: _____

This book reminded me of another book I've read:

_____

_____

_____

_____

_____

_____

Name: _____ Date: _____

Making Connections
Connections to Television

Using my own experiences to help me understand the text

Today I **listened to** the book:

This book reminds me of something I saw on television:

_____

_____

_____

_____

_____

_____

Today I **read** the book: _____

This book reminds me of something I saw on television:

_____

_____

_____

_____

_____

_____

Name: _____ Date: _____

Making Connections
Text-to-Text Connections

Using my own experiences to help me understand the text

Today I **listened to** the book: _____

Use the Venn diagram to compare this book to another book you've read.

Differences   Similarities   Differences

Today I **read** the book: _____

Use the Venn diagram to compare this book to another book you've read.

Differences   Similarities   Differences

Name: _____ Date: _____

Making Connections
Text-to-Self Connections

Using my own experiences to help me understand the text

Today I **listened to** the book: _____

Use the Venn diagram to compare this book to a similar experience you may have had.

Differences   Similarities   Differences

Today I **read** the book: _____

Use the Venn diagram to compare this book to a similar experience you may have had.

Differences   Similarities   Differences

Name: _____ Date: _____

Making Connections
Using a Web

Using my own experiences to help me understand the text

Today I **listened to** the book: _____

Create a web of connections as you listen to the story:

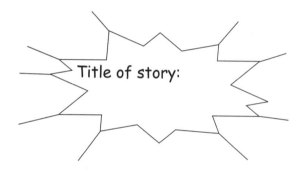

Today I **read** the book: _____

Create a web of connections as you read the story:

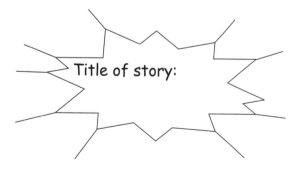

Name: _____ Date: _____

Making Connections
Using an Idea Trail

Using my own experiences to help me understand the text

Today I **listened to** the book: _____

Create an idea trail of connections you can make to the book.

```
┌──────────┐      ┌──────────┐      ┌──────────┐
│          │ ───▶ │          │ ───▶ │          │
│          │      │          │      │          │
└──────────┘      └──────────┘      └──────────┘
                                          │
                                          ▼
┌──────────┐      ┌──────────┐      ┌──────────┐
│          │ ◀─── │          │ ◀─── │          │
│          │      │          │      │          │
└──────────┘      └──────────┘      └──────────┘
```

Today I **read** the book: _____

Create an idea trail of connections you can make to the book.

```
┌──────────┐      ┌──────────┐      ┌──────────┐
│          │ ───▶ │          │ ───▶ │          │
│          │      │          │      │          │
└──────────┘      └──────────┘      └──────────┘
                                          │
                                          ▼
┌──────────┐      ┌──────────┐      ┌──────────┐
│          │ ◀─── │          │ ◀─── │          │
│          │      │          │      │          │
└──────────┘      └──────────┘      └──────────┘
```

Name: _____ Date: _____

Making Connections
Three Types of Connections

Using my own experiences to help me understand the text

Today I **listened to** the book: _____

Using the fishbone diagram, make three different connections to the book.

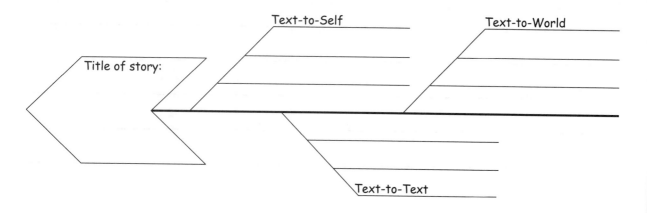

Text-to-Self

Text-to-World

Title of story:

Text-to-Text

Today I **read** the book: _____

Using the fishbone diagram, make three different connections to the book.

Text-to-Self

Text-to-World

Title of story:

Text-to-Text

Name: _____ Date: _____

Making Connections
Valuing Ideas of Others

Using my own experiences to help me understand the text

Today I **listened to** the book: _____

My classmates had good connections. They said...

_____

_____

_____

_____

_____

_____

Today I **read** the book:_____

While I was reading, I found the following connections:

_____

_____

_____

_____

_____

_____

8

Visualizing

"Reading gives us someplace to go when we have to stay where we are."

—*Mason Cooley*

Introduce Visualizing

Introduce the strategy of Visualizing to students. Encourage students to try to make a movie or picture in their mind. Discuss key words or phrases that help us visualize ideas in our minds. The teacher may present a few images for students to practice visualizing: e.g., an ice-cream sundae topped with whipped cream and dripping with hot fudge; the smell from an abandoned gym locker filled with sweaty gym socks and half-eaten snacks. Students should try to utilize all of their senses while visualizing: *What did it look like? Smell like? Feel like?*

Before beginning to read aloud, outline the expectations for the students.

Mental Image

Students use the ideas in the text to create a mental image. While listening, students should draw their image. If they wish, they may include a word or phrase to enhance their image (often students like to add speech bubbles to the images of characters). After reading, encourage students to share their ideas with a partner and explain their rationale for drawing the image they chose.

Use worksheets Visualizing: Mental Image on page 93 and Visualizing: Character on page 94.

Senses

Students focus their attention on sensory cues from the text. They are to listen for clues to how something may smell, sound, feel, or even taste. They should record their ideas on the chart. Creative students may find interesting ways of recording their thinking; however, most students record their ideas with words. After reading, encourage students to share their thinking with a partner.

Use worksheet Visualizing: Senses on page 95.

Multiple Mental Images

Students listen to the text and record things that they are able to visualize. These may include images or sensory cues; e.g., *smelled* rotten beans, or *felt* the hair on the back of my neck stand up. Students may record their ideas in many creative ways (images, words, phrases, etc). After reading, encourage students to share their ideas with a partner.

Use worksheets Visualizing: Using a Fishbone on page 96; Using a Web on page 97; and Using an Idea Trail on page 98.

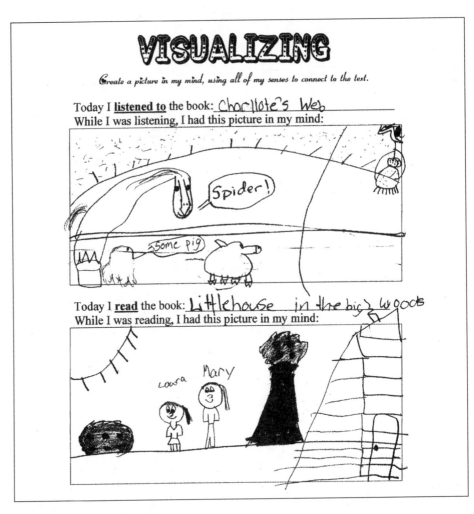

Valuing Ideas of Others

Use worksheet *Visualizing: Valuing Ideas of Others* on page 99.

Students listen to the text and the ideas of their peers to record things that they were able to visualize. During reading, pause occasionally and encourage students to share mental images or senses with a partner or the large group. Students are to represent an idea as described by one of their peers. They may choose to add their own ideas to the representation. After reading, encourage students to share the images that they created with the classmate whose idea inspired their work.

Introduce Independent Reading Activity

Review the strategy of Visualizing with students. Encourage students to share key words, phrases, or descriptions that helped to create vivid images in their minds. Briefly outline the requirements of the task students will complete while reading independently.

Name: _____ Date: _____

Visualizing
Mental Image

Using all my senses to create a mental image of the text

Today I **listened to** the book: _____

While I was listening, I had this picture in my mind:

Today I **read** the book: _____

While I was reading, I had this picture in my mind:

Name: _____ Date: _____

Visualizing
Character

Using all my senses to create a mental image of the text

Today I **listened to** the book: _____

I thought one of the characters might look like this:

Today I **read** the book: _____

I thought one of the characters might look like this:

Name: _____ Date: _____

Visualizing Senses

Using all my senses to create a mental image of the text

Today I **listened to** the book: _____

While I was listening, I could

Hear	Smell	Taste	Feel

Today I **read** the book: _____

While I was reading, I could

Hear	Smell	Taste	Feel

Name: _____ Date: _____

Visualizing
Using a Fishbone

Using all my senses to create a mental image of the text

Today I **listened to** the book: _____

Using the fishbone diagram, draw a picture of four things you were able to visualize while listening to the book.

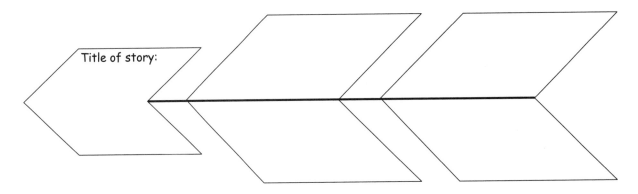

Title of story:

Today I **read** the book: _____

Using the fishbone diagram, draw a picture of four things you were able to visualize while reading the book.

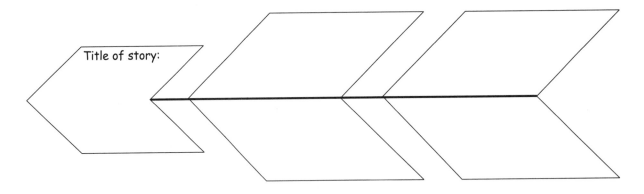

Title of story:

Name: _____ Date: _____

Visualizing
Using a Web

Using all my senses to create a mental image of the text

Today I **listened to** the book: _____

Create a web of things you were able to visualize as you listened to the book.

Today I **read** the book: _____

Create a web of things you were able to visualize as you read the book.

Visualizing
Using an Idea Trail

Using all my senses to create a mental image of the text

Today I **listened to** the book: _____

Create an idea trail of things you were able to visualize as you listened to the book.

```
┌──────────┐      ┌──────────┐      ┌──────────┐
│          │ ───▶ │          │ ───▶ │          │
│          │      │          │      │          │
└──────────┘      └──────────┘      └──────────┘
                                          │
                                          ▼
┌──────────┐      ┌──────────┐      ┌──────────┐
│          │ ◀─── │          │ ◀─── │          │
│          │      │          │      │          │
└──────────┘      └──────────┘      └──────────┘
```

Today I **read** the book:_____

Create an idea trail of things you were able to visualize as you read the book.

```
┌──────────┐      ┌──────────┐      ┌──────────┐
│          │ ───▶ │          │ ───▶ │          │
│          │      │          │      │          │
└──────────┘      └──────────┘      └──────────┘
                                          │
                                          ▼
┌──────────┐      ┌──────────┐      ┌──────────┐
│          │ ◀─── │          │ ◀─── │          │
│          │      │          │      │          │
└──────────┘      └──────────┘      └──────────┘
```

Visualizing
Valuing Ideas of Others

Using all my senses to create a mental image of the text

Today I **listened to** the book: _____

One of my classmates described a good image. This is the way I pictured it as he/she described it.

[ ]

Today I **read** the book:_____

While I was reading, this is an image I had in my mind:

[ ]

9

Asking Questions

"It is not the answers that show us the way, but the questions."

—*Rainer Maria Rilke*

Introduce Asking Questions

Asking questions may be introduced using an introduction like the following:

As effective readers, when we read a book, we have a conversation with the author. There are things that we wonder about, or question, that help us interact with the story. While listening to the story, you'll need to think about what questions you have in your mind.

Before beginning to read aloud, outline the expectations for the students.

While reading with students, pause at certain points that seem to generate interesting questions. Encourage students to record a number of questions from throughout the reading selection. Also, urge students to provide some evidence for their question: e.g., *I wonder if she's moving because, in the picture, she's packing boxes on her car.*

Identifying Questions

Use worksheets *Asking Questions: Wondering* on page 105 and *Asking Questions: Identifying Questions* on page 106.

Students think of questions they have in their mind as listening to the book. These questions may be about the characters, the plot, an element in the book, or something that they found puzzling. Encourage students to record their thinking in a question. At first, they may find it helpful to begin with a prompt: "I was wondering…" Pausing during reading and encouraging students to share their questions with a partner will allow them to articulate their questions before having to record them. They may also benefit from the ideas of their peers. Although it is difficult, refrain from answering students' questions—especially the obvious ones; however, if students are able to determine the answer to their questions, encourage them to record these as well.

ASKING QUESTIONS

Asking questions and searching for answers: before during and after reading.

Today I **listened to** the book: ___Bees___

Three questions I would love to ask the author about this book are:

1. Why do bees buzz aroud?

2. How do bees get the nectar from the flowers?

3. How do bees put the honey into the hive?

Today I **read** the book: ___Turtles___

Three questions I would love to ask the author about this book are:

1. What kind of food do turtles eat?

2. How do land turtles pull their head and legs into their shells.

3. Do sea turtles HYE-bur-nate?

Before, During, and After

Use worksheets *Asking Questions: Before Listening or Reading* on page 107; *During Listening or Reading* on page 108; *After Listening or Reading* on page 109; and *Before, During, and After* on page 110.

Students record the questions they think of at varying stages of reading the text. Instructions may be similar to the following:

We're going to focus on the things we think about before, during, and after we hear a book. As we learn more about a text our questions change. And even when the book is finished, sometimes we still have questions that remain unanswered

- Begin by examining the cover of the book and encouraging students to share their initial thoughts and questions about the book. Then flip slowly through the illustrations, inviting students to share their questions.
- During reading, pause at key points and encourage students to share and record their questions.
- After reading, revisit the illustrations by leafing back through the text: *Sometimes when we read a book, we have more questions after we've read it than before. Maybe our questions are about different things.* Encourage students to take a few moments to record the questions and ideas that they have now that the book is finished.

ASKING QUESTIONS

Asking questions and searching for answers: before during and after reading.

Today I **listened to** the book: Amelia's Road

Before I heard the book, I was wondering:	While I was listening, I was wondering:	After listening, I was wondering:
why does it say Amelas road when she is in a field with crops? IS she moving?	why does Amela hate roads? maybe she hates roads because she travels too much. why does Amela like the tree? why does Amela call the road called the Accidental road?	Does Amelia leave the box as a sigh that she has been here before?

Today I **read** the book: The End Of The Beginning

Before I read the book, I was wondering:	While I was reading, I was wondering:	After reading, I was wondering:
IS Avon going to have another fight with another Snail because Avon had a fight with an oddly dressed snail I wonder if Edward is going to get into a fight with another ant.	while I was reading I was wondering if they are going to encount a dragon? I think they might encounter a deadly animal?	After reading I was wondering if they are going to get another group member?

Characters in Fiction

Use worksheet *Asking Questions: Characters in Fiction* on page 111.

Students record questions they want to ask the characters in the story. They may choose to ask one character a number of questions, or ask a different question of each character. After reading, it may be fun for the students to "interview" their classmates in role as the characters in the story.

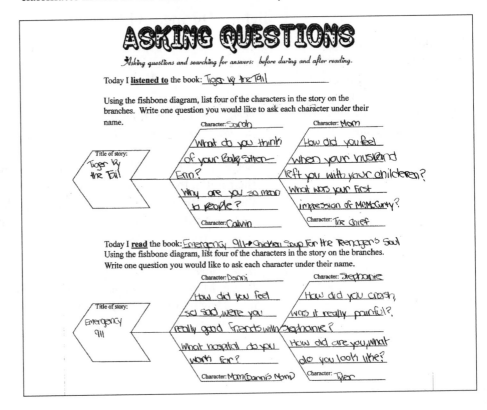

Question Trail

Use worksheet *Asking Questions: Question Trail* on page 112.

Students record the questions they have while listening. Using the idea trail, students can record questions for characters, questions for the author, or "wonderings" they have, and include answers to their questions as they are revealed to them. During and after reading, encourage students to share their questions with a partner.

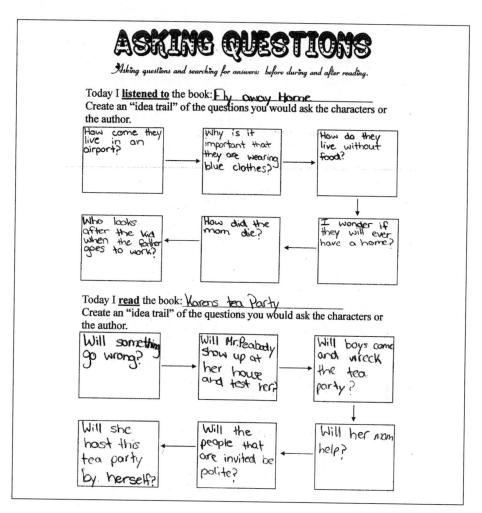

Valuing Ideas of Others

Use worksheet *Asking Questions: Valuing Ideas of Others* on page 113.

Students share their questions with each other while listening to the book. It is important to pause occasionally and encourage students to share their ideas with partners or with the large group. Students should record questions from their peers that they think are interesting or valuable. They may choose to include answers to the questions that become apparent. After reading, encourage students to share the questions they recorded with the student who asked it.

Introduce Independent Reading Activity

Review the strategy of Asking Questions and the task that students will complete on their own. If students discover the answers to questions that they have recorded, encourage them to write them as well.

Name: _____ Date: _____

Asking Questions
Wondering

Asking questions and trying to find the answers—before, during, and after listening or reading

Today I **listened to** the book: _____

While I was listening I was confused about...

_____

_____

_____

_____

_____

_____

Today I **read** the book: _____

While I was reading I was confused about...

_____

_____

_____

_____

_____

_____

Name: _____ Date: _____

Asking Questions
Identifying Questions

Asking questions and trying to find the answers—before, during, and after listening or reading

Today I **listened to** the book: _____

Three questions I would like to ask the author about the book:

1. _____

_____

2. _____

_____

3. _____

_____

Today I **read** the book: _____

Three questions I would like to ask the author about the book:

1. _____

_____

2. _____

_____

3. _____

_____

Name: _____ Date: _____

Asking Questions
Before Listening or Reading

Asking questions and trying to find the answers—before, during, and after listening or reading

Today I **listened to** the book: _____

Before I heard the book I was wondering...

- _____
- _____
- _____
- _____

Today I **read** the book: _____

Before I read the book, I was wondering...

- _____
- _____
- _____
- _____

Name: _____ Date: _____

Asking Questions
During Listening or Reading

Asking questions and trying to find the answers—before, during, and after listening or reading

Today I **listened to** the book:

While I was listening I was wondering…

- _____
- _____
- _____
- _____

Today I **read** the book:

While I was reading I was wondering…

- _____
- _____
- _____
- _____

Name: _____ Date: _____

Asking Questions
After Listening or Reading

Asking questions and trying to find the answers—before, during, and after listening or reading

Today I **listened to** the book:

After I heard the book, I was wondering...

- _____

- _____

- _____

- _____

Today I **read** the book:

After I **read** the book, I was wondering...

- _____

- _____

- _____

- _____

Name: _____ Date: _____

Asking Questions
Before, During, and After

Asking questions and trying to find the answers—before, during, and after listening or reading

Today I **listened to** the book: _____

Before I heard the book, I was wondering:	While I was listening, I was wondering:	After listening, I was wondering:

Today I **read** the book: _____

Before I read the book, I was wondering:	While I was reading, I was wondering:	After reading, I was wondering:

Name: _____ Date: _____

Asking Questions
Characters in Fiction

Asking questions and trying to find the answers—before, during, and after listening or reading

Today I **listened to** the book: _____
Using the fishbone diagram, list the characters in the story and write one question you would like to ask each character.

Character: _____   Character: _____

Title of story:

Character: _____   Character: _____

Today I **read** the book: _____
Using the fishbone diagram, list the characters in the story and write one question you would like to ask each character.

Character: _____   Character: _____

Title of story:

Character: _____   Character: _____

Name: _____ Date: _____

Asking Questions
Question Trail

Asking questions and trying to find the answers—before, during, and after listening or reading

Today I **listened to** the book: _____
Create an idea trail of the questions you would ask the characters or the author.

```
┌──────────┐      ┌──────────┐      ┌──────────┐
│          │ ───▶ │          │ ───▶ │          │
└──────────┘      └──────────┘      └──────────┘
                                          │
                                          ▼
┌──────────┐      ┌──────────┐      ┌──────────┐
│          │ ◀─── │          │ ◀─── │          │
└──────────┘      └──────────┘      └──────────┘
```

Today I **read** the book:_____
Create an idea trail of the questions you would ask the characters or the author.

```
┌──────────┐      ┌──────────┐      ┌──────────┐
│          │ ───▶ │          │ ───▶ │          │
└──────────┘      └──────────┘      └──────────┘
                                          │
                                          ▼
┌──────────┐      ┌──────────┐      ┌──────────┐
│          │ ◀─── │          │ ◀─── │          │
└──────────┘      └──────────┘      └──────────┘
```

Name: _____ Date: _____

Asking Questions
Valuing Ideas of Others

Asking questions and trying to find the answers—before, during, and after listening or reading

Today I **listened to** the book:

My classmates asked good questions. They asked…

- _____

- _____

- _____

- _____

Today I **read** the book:

While I was reading I was curious about…

- _____

- _____

- _____

- _____

10

Synthesizing

> "Knowledge without the ability to think is a total waste, like words written in a book that is never read."
>
> —*F. Vice*

Introduce Synthesizing

Begin with an introduction or review of Synthesizing. This may include a brief introduction or time for students to share and refresh their memories with a partner. If you are introducing Synthesizing for the first time, students may require a little more in-depth introduction as well as repeated practice to completely master synthesis. This is one of the more complicated strategies for students to fully understand, so be patient and allow many opportunities for students to practice their skills.

Before beginning to read aloud, outline the expectations for the students.

The teacher may use the "ripple in the pond" analogy (Miller, 2002)—see pages 26–27—to help students create a visual image of synthesizing. Synthesis is really the evolution of thought. It is important for students to recognize that our thoughts evolve, changing or growing through time and experience.

Summarizing

Use worksheet *Synthesizing: Summarizing* on page 119.

Students listen to the text and create a summary of the main ideas. Recalling the text using their own words encourages students to paraphrase the concepts in the text. After recording their summaries, it is beneficial for students to share their summaries with a partner or with the large group.

Retell

Use worksheet *Synthesizing: Retell* on page 120.

Students listen to the text and record the main ideas or events in the text. After reading, students should use their notes to retell the book to a partner. Recording the main ideas is really using the strategy of Determining Important Ideas (and the students may inform you as such), but it is the retelling—using their own words and phrases, introducing their own thinking into the text—that makes this a synthesizing activity. Encouraging students to retell orally is much more effective than requiring a written retell. The oral component of the retell allows students to creatively interpret the text, as well as listen to and learn from the synthesises of their peers.

SYNTHESIZING

Combining new ideas with what I already know to get something new and different.

Today I <u>**listened to**</u> the book: _Jillan Jiggs to the Rescue_

While you are listening, jot down a few notes so that you can retell the story to a partner.

- The little sister was crying
- she thought there was a monster
- they built a monster machine
- they went to the forest to find it
- they heard a rattle
- they cooked monster bait
- it was a cat

Today I <u>**read**</u> the book: _The Snack attack mystery_

While you are reading, jot down a few notes so that you can retell the story to a partner.

- they find a clue
- theyare going to find out how the snacks gone
- theycant find the thief
- they thought it was the kindergarteners
- they had gerbils
- the gerbils had eaten the snacks

Recording Important Ideas

Use worksheets *Synthesizing: What to Remember* on page 121 and *Synthesizing: Important Ideas* on page 122.

Students listen to the text and record ideas that they think are important to remember. Some of these may be ideas from the text, but others may be ideas that the students think of as they are listening. Encouraging students to record their own thinking in addition to the ideas from the text is an important component of these activities. The teacher may pause during reading to allow time for the students to reflect on the ideas from the text and their own thinking, and record their ideas. As always, sharing their thinking with a partner helps students clarify their thoughts and value the ideas of others.

Reflecting on Initial Ideas

Use worksheet *Synthesizing: Reflecting on Initial Ideas* on page 123.

At the beginning of the read-aloud, students are to record their thinking. This may be an opinion, prior knowledge, a prediction, or any other important idea that they may have about the text. As they listen to the text, if their ideas are altered (strengthened, changed, expanded on, etc.), the students can write these new insights in the second box. Encourage students to reflect on their initial perceptions as a basis for their subsequent ideas. After reading, allow time for students to verbalize their thoughts by sharing with a partner; e.g., "At the beginning I thought… but later I realized…"

Alternate Ending

Use worksheet *Synthesizing: Alternate Ending* on page 124.

Students listen to the text and think of a different ending for the book. Using their existing knowledge and creative ideas, students should take a few minutes after reading to compose an alternate ending. Younger students may prefer to share their thinking orally with a partner, and older students may choose to make notes and share their expanded ideas orally.

SYNTHESIZING

Combining new ideas with what I already know to get something new and different.

Today I **listened to** the book: _Something might be Hiding_

If I were the author, I would have ended the story like this:

The monster came out of the furnace and took the matchbox and whispered in Jenny's ear "Good bye". Then when the monster sat in the woods he went to bed in the matchbox.

Today I **read** the book: _Pippi on the Run_

If I were the author, I would have ended the story like this:

I would end the story like this: When they come back from their adventure they ask their mom and dad if they could have a picnic togeter with Pippi. They would say yes. After they finish eating they ran in the forset and got lost. Their adventure started all over again.

The Big Picture

Use worksheets *Synthesizing: Using an Arrow Graphic* on page 125 and *Synthesizing: Using a Lightbulb Graphic* on page 126.

These graphic organizers clearly represent the process of synthesizing. As students are listening, they record their initial "big idea" in the first image (arrow or lightbulb). As they continue to listen, their ideas may grow or change. As they have new ideas that build on their initial idea, they record them in the subsequent images. After reading, students could share their thinking with a partner; e.g., "I initially thought… then I discovered… Finally I concluded…"

Puzzle

Use worksheet *Synthesizing: Puzzle* on page 127.

Students listen to the text and try to determine the clues that fit together to form a complete story. One might introduce this activity in the following way:

Often readers need to figure out a number of clues, or pieces of a puzzle, while reading. Some authors give the reader hints about a story, and it's up to us to put it all together to completely understand the story. This is called Synthesizing. As effective synthesizers, we listen critically for important clues, and then put them together to form a new and complete picture of the story.

As you are listening, you need to listen carefully for clues about the story. If you hear a clue (or something that you think is an important hint), record your thinking. When you think you have all the clues, try to put them together in your mind.

Text selection is important with this activity: it works well with a text that has a problem or mystery to solve. Placing emphasis on or reviewing clues with students will help them all have an "ah-ha" moment or epiphany—the fantastic moment in literature when it all becomes clear. Encouraging students to share with partners will help all students find clues, as they work cooperatively to enable each other to find clues that they may have missed working on their own. After reading, encourage students to discuss their thoughts and share the clues that lead to their conclusion. It is interesting to flip back through the story to find the clues that might have been overlooked the first time through.

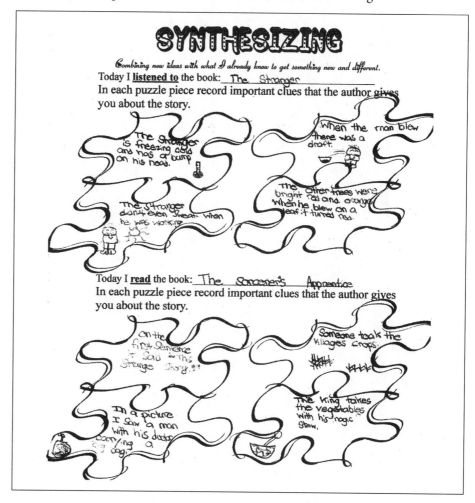

Valuing Ideas of Others

Use worksheet *Synthesizing: Valuing Ideas of Others* on page 128.

While reading, pause often to encourage students to share their thinking with partners or with the large group. As students hear ideas that they think are good ideas, they should record them. After reading, it is interesting for students to share the ideas they recorded, as well as the source; e.g., "I think Matthew had a good idea. He said…" This enables students to learn from the ideas of others and to recognize that other students appreciate and value their ideas.

Introduce Independent Reading Activity

Before beginning independent reading, review the skill of Synthesizing. For example: *As synthesizers we are thinking about our ideas and how they may change as we continue to learn more from the book.* While students are reading on their own, they are to practice the strategy that was modelled and practiced during the read-aloud.

Name: _____ Date: _____

Synthesizing
Summarizing

Reflecting on the text and the ways my thoughts have evolved or changed

Today I **listened to** the book: _____

The book was about...

_____

_____

_____

_____

_____

_____

Today I **read** the book: _____

The book was about...

_____

_____

_____

_____

_____

_____

Synthesizing
Retell

Reflecting on the text and the ways my thoughts have evolved or changed

Today I **listened to** the book: _____

While you are listening, jot down a few notes so that you can retell the book to a partner.

- _____
- _____
- _____
- _____
- _____
- _____

Today I **read** the book: _____

While you are reading, jot down a few notes so that you can retell the book to a partner.

- _____
- _____
- _____
- _____
- _____
- _____

Name: _____ Date: _____

Synthesizing
What to Remember

Reflecting on the text and the ways my thoughts have evolved or changed

Today I **listened to** the book: _____

While I was listening, I thought it was important to remember…

- _____

- _____

- _____

- _____

- _____

- _____

Today I **read** the book: _____

While I was reading, I thought it was important to remember…

- _____

- _____

- _____

- _____

- _____

- _____

Name: _____ Date: _____

Synthesizing
Important Ideas

Reflecting on the text and the ways my thoughts have evolved or changed

Today I **listened to** the book: _____

While I was listening, I had the following ideas:

- _____

- _____

- _____

- _____

- _____

- _____

Today I **read** the book: _____

While I was reading, I had the following ideas:

- _____

- _____

- _____

- _____

- _____

- _____

Name: _____ Date: _____

Synthesizing
Reflecting on Initial Ideas

Reflecting on the text and the ways my thoughts have evolved or changed

Today I **listened to** the book: _____

Before I heard the book I thought...	After I heard the book I thought...

Today I **read** the book: _____

Before I read the book I thought...	After I read the book I thought...

Name: _____ Date: _____

Synthesizing
Alternate Ending

Reflecting on the text and the ways my thoughts have evolved or changed

Today I **listened to** the book: _____

If I were the author, I would have ended the book like this:

_____

_____

_____

_____

_____

_____

_____

Today I **read** the book: _____

If I were the author, I would have ended the book like this:

_____

_____

_____

_____

_____

_____

_____

Name: _____ Date: _____

Synthesizing
Using an Arrow Graphic

Reflecting on the text and the ways my thoughts have evolved or changed

Today I **listened to** the book: _____
While you are listening, show your first "big idea" in the first arrow. As you continue to listen, your ideas might change or grow. Record your new ideas in the next arrows.

Today I **read** the book: _____
While you are reading, show your first "big idea" in the first arrow. As you continue to read, your ideas might change or grow. Record your new ideas in the next arrows.

Synthesizing
Using a Lightbulb Graphic

Reflecting on the text and the ways my thoughts have evolved or changed

Today I **listened to** the book: _____
While you are listening, show your first "big idea" in the lightbulb. As you continue to listen, your ideas might change or grow. Record your new ideas on the rays coming from the lightbulb.

Today I **read** the book: _____
While you are reading, show your first "big idea" in the lightbulb. As you continue to read, your ideas might change or grow. Record your new ideas on the rays coming from the lightbulb.

Name: _____ Date: _____

Synthesizing
Puzzle

Reflecting on the text and the ways my thoughts have evolved or changed

Today I **listened to** the book: _____

In each puzzle piece, record important clues that the author gives you about the story.

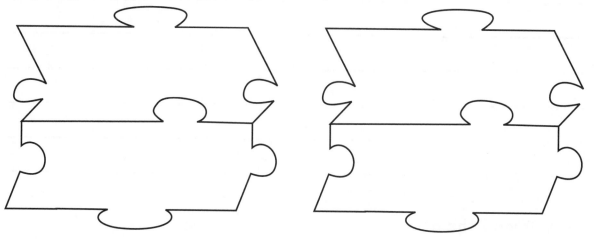

Today I **read** the book: _____

In each puzzle piece, record important clues that the author gives you about the story.

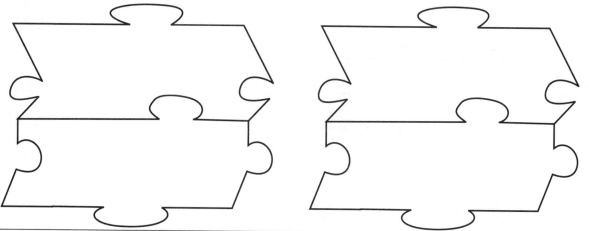

Name: _____ Date: _____

Synthesizing
Valuing Ideas of Others

Reflecting on the text and the ways my thoughts have evolved or changed

Today I **listened to** the book: _____

While I was listening, my classmates had some good ideas. They said...

- _____

- _____

- _____

- _____

- _____

- _____

Today I **read** the book:

While I was reading, I had the following ideas:

- _____

- _____

- _____

- _____

- _____

- _____

11

Integrated Metacognition

"In the final analysis it is not what you do for your children but what you have taught them to do for themselves that will make them successful."

—*Ann Landers*

Introduce Integrated Metacognition

Before beginning to read aloud, outline the expectations for the students.

Begin with an introduction or review of Integrated Metacognition. As students master the comprehension strategies in isolation, they will automatically being to find the ways their new skills work together. This integration of the strategies is the goal.

Begin the lesson with a review of all of the metacognitive strategies. This could be a quick overview, since students will probably be quite familiar with all of them. For example, you might say *There are seven strategies that we should use while thinking about books.* Encourage students to respond by naming all seven strategies and coming up with a one-sentence description of each: e.g., Visualizing—creating a mental image of the book; Predicting—using the clues from to story to make a guess about what might happen next; etc. Effective readers use all of these strategies together.

Putting the Strategies Together

Use worksheet *Integrated Metacognition: Using a Fishbone* on page 132; *Using a Table* on page 133; *Using the Six-Strategy Chart* on page 134; *Using a Web* on page 135; and *Using an Idea Trail* on page 136.

All of the Integrated Metacognition activities focus on the same skills. As students use the various graphic organizers to record their thinking, they will become more able to alternate between the strategies and effectively classify their thoughts into the appropriate categories. Encourage students to record their ideas while listening using a variety of the graphic organizers. They should try to identify the strategy that most accurately describes their ideas. Encourage students to record their ideas in a variety of ways (pictures, words, phrases, etc.). During reading, pause to encourage students to discuss their ideas with partners and with the large group.

INTEGRATED METACOGNITION
Using all of the strategies to understand the text.

Today I **listened to** the book: Something Beautiful.

Create a Fishbone that shows the thoughts you had while listening. Write one strategy on each branch, and describe your idea under it.

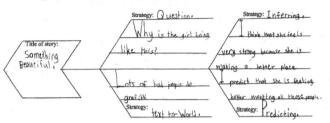

Title of story: Something Beautiful.

Strategy: Question.
Why is the girl living like this?

Strategy: Inferring.
I think that she feels very strong because she is making a better place.

Strategy: text to-World.
Lots of bad people do grafitti.

Strategy: Predicting.
I predict that she is feeling better meeting all those people.

Today I **read** the book: Dinosaur.

Create a Fishbone that shows the thoughts you had while listening. Write one strategy on each branch, and describe your idea under it.

Title of story: dinosaur.

Strategy: Question.
What's an Iguanadon?

Strategy: Inferring.
I infer that the mother iguanadon is getting annoyed.

strategy: predicts
I predict that the parcasaurolophus will come back

Strategy: Visualizing.
The 12 egg's that are in the nest.

INTEGRATED METACOGNITION
Using all of the strategies to understand the text.

Today I **listened to** the book: My Great Aunt Arizona

As I was listening, I was thinking about my thinking. This is how I used each of the strategies:

Making Inferences:	Making Predictions:	Making Connections:
I'm guessing Arizona will became a very good teacher.	I predict that Arizona will go everywhere in the world.	Arizona and I are both alike. We both love singing, reading, and dancing. We also dream.
Determining Important Ideas:	**Visualizing:**	**Synthesizing:**
Jim is Arizona's brother. Arizona's mom died. Her dad got married.	I visualized the brown fiddle with Arizona dancing. I also visualized Arizona saying to the class only in my head.	I understand that Arizona has a good life. She has a family but her mom died.

Today I **read** the book: The Rainbow Fish

As I was reading, I was thinking about my thinking. This is how I used each of the strategies:

Making Inferences:	Making Predictions:	Making Connections:
I'm guessing Rainbow Fish would be happier if she shared.	I predict that Rainbow Fish will share.	Rainbow fish and I are both gorgeous!
Determining Important Ideas:	**Visualizing:**	**Synthesizing:**
Rainbow fish is popular and greedy.	I visualized the beautiful tropical, colourful, beautiful fish.	I understand Rainbow fish loves Herself.

Introduce Independent Reading Activity

Before beginning independent reading, review the skill of Integrated Metacognition.

As effective readers, we need to think about all of the strategies working together. As you are reading, think about your thinking and try to record some of the ideas you have. If you make a prediction, try to record it and remember to label it Prediction. You may not use all seven strategies, but try to include a variety of them.

While students are reading on their own, they practice the strategy that was modelled and practiced during the read-aloud.

Name: _____ Date: _____

Integrated Metacognition
Using a Fishbone

Using all the strategies to understand the text

Today I **listened to** the book: _____

Create a fishbone that shows the thoughts you had while listening. Write one strategy on each branch, and record your idea under it.

Strategy: _____   Strategy: _____

Title of story:

Strategy: _____   Strategy: _____

Today I **read** the book: _____

Create a fishbone that shows the thoughts you had while reading. Write one strategy on each branch, and record your idea under it.

Strategy: _____   Strategy: _____

Title of story:

Strategy: _____   Strategy: _____

Name: _____ Date: _____

Integrated Metacognition
Using a Table

Using all the strategies to understand the text

Today I **listened to** the book: _____

As I was listening, I was thinking about my thinking. This is how I used each of the strategies:

Making Inferences:	Making Predictions:	Making Connections:
Determining Important Ideas:	Visualizing:	Synthesizing:

Today I **read** the book: _____

As I was reading, I was thinking about my thinking. This is how I used each of the strategies:

Making Inferences	Making Predictions:	Making Connections:
Determining Important Ideas:	Visualizing:	Synthesizing:

Name: _____ Date: _____

Integrated Metacognition
Using the Six-Strategy Chart

Using all the strategies to understand the text

Today I **listened to** the book: _____

As I was listening, I was thinking about my thinking. These are the strategies I used and the ways I used them:

Strategy:_____	Strategy:_____	Strategy:_____
	Title of Book:	
Strategy:_____	Strategy:_____	Strategy:_____

Today I **read** the book: _____

As I was reading, I was thinking about my thinking. These are the strategies I used and the ways I used them.

Strategy:_____	Strategy:_____	Strategy:_____
	Title of Book:	
Strategy:_____	Strategy:_____	Strategy:_____

Name: _____ Date: _____

Integrated Metacognition
Using a Web

Using all the strategies to understand the text

Today I **listened** to the book: _____

Create a web that shows the thoughts you had while listening. For each idea, write down the strategy you used: Making Inferences, Making Predictions, Determining Important Information, Making Connections, Visualizing, Asking Questions, or Synthesizing.

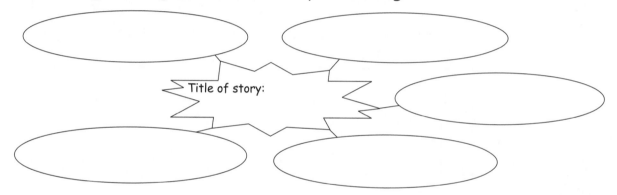

Today I **read** the book: _____
Create a web that shows the thoughts you had while reading. For each idea, write down the strategy you used: Making Inferences, Making Predictions, Determining Important Information, Making Connections, Visualizing, Asking Questions, or Synthesizing.

Name: _____ Date: _____

Integrated Metacognition
Using an Idea Trail

Using all the strategies to understand the text

Today I **listened to** the book: _____
Create an idea trail that shows the thoughts you had while listening.
For each idea, write down the strategy you used: Making Inferences,
Making Predictions, Determining Important Information, Making
Connections, Visualizing, Asking Questions, or Synthesizing.

```
┌──────────┐      ┌──────────┐      ┌──────────┐
│          │ ───▶ │          │ ───▶ │          │
└──────────┘      └──────────┘      └──────────┘
                                          │
                                          ▼
┌──────────┐      ┌──────────┐      ┌──────────┐
│          │ ◀─── │          │ ◀─── │          │
└──────────┘      └──────────┘      └──────────┘
```

Today I **read** the book: _____
Create an idea trail that shows the thoughts you had while reading. For
each idea, write down the strategy you used: Making Inferences,
Making Predictions, Determining Important Information, Making
Connections, Visualizing, Asking Questions, or Synthesizing.

```
┌──────────┐      ┌──────────┐      ┌──────────┐
│          │ ───▶ │          │ ───▶ │          │
└──────────┘      └──────────┘      └──────────┘
                                          │
                                          ▼
┌──────────┐      ┌──────────┐      ┌──────────┐
│          │ ◀─── │          │ ◀─── │          │
└──────────┘      └──────────┘      └──────────┘
```

12

Assessment

"'I can't do it' never yet accomplished anything; 'I will try' has performed wonders."

—George P. Burnham

Having collected all of this work from your students, the logical question is "What do I DO with it?" As a busy teacher, I am hesitant to embrace any new procedure that appears to include an ominous amount of marking. Guided Listening is structured

- to incorporate the marking time right into your instructional day
- to provide immediate feedback to your students
- to assist in grouping students for further instruction
- and to compile assessments for reporting purposes

The Guided Listening worksheets are divided into two parts: an instructional time followed by independent practice. Why not use this independent reading time to mark the previous day's work? This way, marking is built right into the instructional day, and teachers have the opportunity to conference with students about the previous day's work if necessary.

Guided Listening provides tangible, ongoing, consistent feedback to students about their progress in metacognition of reading strategies. Teachers have regular evaluative results for reporting and direct instruction in oral language and independent reading. In the past, these have probably been two of the hardest areas of the curriculum to assess accurately and fairly. Guided Listening targets these difficult areas with amazing efficiency. The class tracking sheets have been designed for efficient recording, summarizing, and use of students' progress. These marks are easily utilized for many purposes, including writing student progress report cards.

Rubrics

Each set of student worksheets targets a specific set of skills within the reading strategy. Teachers have the option of focusing on one or two specific metacognitive strategies at a time—having students work toward mastery of a few skills at a time or on a number of strategies, encouraging a balance and full range of oral listening and independent reading skills. The targeted skills are noted beside the four-point rubric, which correlates with the class tracking sheets. This provides an effective way of cross-referencing and recording students' progress. It then becomes easy to transfer this information from the class tracking sheets to student progress report cards.

Each comprehension strategy is matched with a corresponding rubric. Each rubric has two components. The top half of the rubric is intended to assess the student's oral language skills as they were using these skills to listen for and record their ideas. The bottom half addresses the transfer of these skills as students worked to complete the activity with their independent reading.

Each rubric addresses a different set of skills, for both oral language and independent reading. As you work your way through the strategies and use a variety of rubrics, different skill sets will be assessed.

Class Tracking

Class tracking sheets are designed for teachers as at-a-glance summaries of an individual student's progress in each of the strategy areas, in both oral language and independent reading.

Class tracking sheets (pages 147–154) are designed to make it easy to collect, organize, and interpret student data. Each metacognitive strategy is recorded on a separate class tracking sheet. This allows you to observe an individual student's progress over time and further guide direct instruction.

Tracking sheets are divided into two areas for each strategy: oral language skills, and independent reading skills. These areas are reported on separately, although through Guided Listening they are taught together. An area is provided for teachers to compile students' marks in these areas separately, and record an overall mark.

These tracking sheets make it very easy to group students according to their individual needs. For example, you may notice that six of your students are consistently struggling with Determining Important Information. By placing these students together for a guided reading session, you would be able to support their needs by providing more direct instruction and practice in the area they need it most. In the same manner, if you noticed that a group of students were consistently successful with Making Inferences, then they may be grouped together. Perhaps this group of students would benefit from a more challenging text, one that requires the reader to make a great number of inferences (maybe a mystery story would appeal to them).

Targeted skills are clearly outlined on the top of each tracking sheet and can be transferred directly to student progress reports.

The goal of teaching is to be constantly moving our students forward. In order to move them, we need to know where they are! By tracking students on the class list, teachers have a quick reference as to which strategies each student is successful with, and which need strengthening.

Implications for Instruction

Oral language skills and independent reading are generally very difficult areas to assess accurately, fairly, and consistently. It is difficult to track students progress in these areas. Guided Listening allows for quick, regular assessment of students' metacognitive processes while they are listening and independently reading. Through regular monitoring of students' progress, the teacher is able to use this information to focus instruction.

- By analyzing students' strengths and needs, students may be grouped into guided reading groups to provide small-group and individualized instruction on specific strategies.
- Teachers are able to target specific strategies and use teaching time for focused, purposeful instruction to move students forward.
- Regular monitoring provides consistent, ongoing assessment and feedback to students about their progress toward mastery of metacognitive reading strategies.

Name: _____ Date: _____

Rubric: Making Inferences

	SKILLS	Level 1	Level 2	Level 3	Level 4
Oral Language	**Make inferences about oral texts using stated and implied ideas from the texts as evidence.**	Ideas seem unrelated to stated and implied evidence in the text.	Ideas are somewhat logical and connected to stated and implied evidence in the text.	Ideas are thoughtful and connected to stated and implied evidence in the text.	Ideas are thoughtful and supported by stated and implied evidence in the text.
	Consider the ideas of others while making inferences and drawing conclusions.	The ideas of others are rarely considered.	The ideas of others are somewhat considered.	The ideas of others are considered and used as a basis for further thought.	The ideas of others are thoughtfully considered and used to effectively draw conclusions.
	Evaluate oral texts using ideas presented in the texts.	Few ideas from the text are considered or used as a basis for student's evaluation (likes and dislikes).	Ideas in text are somewhat considered and may be used as a basis for student's evaluation (likes and dislikes).	Ideas in texts are considered and used as a basis for student's evaluation (likes and dislikes).	Ideas in texts are thoughtfully considered and used as a basis for student's evaluation (likes and dislikes) of the text.
Independent Reading	**Identify theme or main idea of texts.**	Theme is not clearly identified or is not supported by main ideas of the text.	Theme is somewhat identified and is partially supported by main ideas of the text.	Theme is identified and is supported with some evidence from the text.	Theme is clearly identified and thoroughly supported with evidence from the text.
	Use evidence from texts to infer feelings/ emotions of characters.	Main characters' feelings are not identified; little or no evidence from the text is provided.	Main characters' feelings are somewhat described using stated and implied evidence from the text.	Main characters' feelings are described using stated and implied evidence from the text.	Main characters' feelings are clearly described using stated and implied evidence from the text.
	Identify the point of view presented in texts and suggest possible alternative perspectives.	Point of view and alternative perspectives are unclear.	Point of view is discussed and alternative perspectives considered.	Point of view is thoughtfully discussed and alternative perspectives considered.	Point of view is thoughtfully discussed and alternative perspectives considered based on evidence from the text.

Name: _____ Date: _____

Rubric: Making Predictions

	SKILLS	Level 1	Level 2	Level 3	Level 4
Oral Language	**Apply listening strategies effectively to make predictions while listening.**	Predictions have few connections to information presented in the text.	Predictions are somewhat reasonable and based on some information presented in the text.	Predictions are reasonable and based on information presented in the text.	Predictions are well developed and supported by information presented in the text.
	Revise predictions as new information is heard.	Little new information is included, or information is unrelated to initial prediction.	Some new information included is related to initial prediction.	New information included is relevant and related to initial prediction.	New information included is relevant and related to initial prediction and new ideas from the text.
	Evaluate predictions as new information is presented.	Evaluation of predictions is unclear or unrelated to the text.	Evaluation of predictions is somewhat reasonable and based on evidence presented in the text or original ideas.	Evaluation of predictions is reasonable and based on evidence presented in the text or creative original ideas.	Evaluation of predictions is well thought-out and based on evidence presented in the text or creative original ideas.
Independent Reading	**Make reasonable predictions based on evidence presented in the text.**	Predictions are unclear or not supported by the text.	Predictions are somewhat based on the text.	Predictions are reasonable and based on the text.	Predictions are creative, well developed, and supported by the text.
	Reassess predictions as new information is read.	Predictions are not revised or reassessed as new information is read.	Predictions are partially revised as new information is read.	Predictions are logically assessed and revised accordingly.	Predictions are logically assessed as new information is thoughtfully considered.
	Provide evidence from the text to support predictions.	Little or no evidence to support predictions.	Predictions are somewhat supported by evidence from the text.	Predictions are supported by evidence from the text.	Predictions are clearly supported by evidence from the text.

Name: _____ Date: _____

Rubric: Determining Important Ideas

	SKILLS	Level 1	Level 2	Level 3	Level 4
Oral Language	**Listen critically to gather information from a variety of sources.**	Few key ideas and little important information from class discussion and text are recorded.	Some key ideas and important information from class discussion and text are recorded.	Most of the key ideas and important information from class discussion and text are recorded.	All of the key ideas and important information from class discussion and text are recorded.
	Reflect on learning/ thinking while listening.	Student rarely uses existing knowledge and information from the text to determine important ideas and to revise his/her thinking accordingly.	Student sometimes uses existing knowledge and information from the text to determine important ideas and may revise his/her thinking accordingly.	Student uses existing knowledge and information from the text to determine important ideas and revises his/her thinking accordingly.	Student thoughtfully uses existing knowledge and information from the text to determine important ideas and revises his/her thinking accordingly.
Independent Reading	**Identify important information, ideas, and supporting details in texts.**	Few key ideas and important information from the text are recorded.	Some key ideas and important information from the text are recorded.	Most of the key ideas and important information from the text are recorded.	All of the key ideas and important information from the text are recorded.
	Sequence important information, ideas, and supporting details in texts.	Few key ideas and important information from the text are recorded; may be sequenced incorrectly.	Some key ideas and important information from the text are sequenced correctly.	Most of the key ideas and important information from the text are sequenced correctly.	All of the key ideas and important information from the text are sequenced correctly.
	Summarize important ideas.	Few of the important ideas are included in a summary of the text.	Some of the important ideas are included in a summary of the text.	Most of the important ideas are included in a logical summary of the text.	All of the important ideas are included in a creative summary of the text.

Name: _____ Date: _____

Rubric: Making Connections

	SKILLS	Level 1	Level 2	Level 3	Level 4
Oral Language	**Record a variety of connections while listening to oral texts.**	Few connections were recorded.	Some connections were recorded.	Many connections were recorded.	Many connections of a variety of types (text-to-text, text-to-self, text-to-world) were recorded.
	Demonstrate respect for peers while listening to the ideas of others.	Respect rarely shown by listening to the ideas of peers and by responding with appropriate feedback.	Respect sometimes shown by listening to the ideas of peers and occasionally responding appropriately with positive feedback.	Respect shown by listening attentively to the ideas of peers and responding appropriately with positive feedback.	Respect shown by listening attentively to the ideas of peers and responding appropriately with positive feedback; ideas of peers are sometimes considered as a basis for new connections to the text.
Independent Reading	**Record text-to-text, text-to-self and text-to-world connections.**	Few connections are recorded.	Some connections are recorded.	A variety of connections are recorded.	A variety of connections are recorded and clearly linked to passages from the text.
	Use personal experiences to form connections to a variety of texts.	Few personal experiences are described; connections to text may be unclear.	Personal experiences are described and somewhat connect to text.	Personal experiences are described and used as a basis for connections to text.	Personal experiences are described, clearly connect to text, and enhance students' understanding of the text.
	Identify similarities and differences between texts and personal experiences.	Few similarities and differences between text and personal experiences are described.	Some similarities and differences between text and personal experiences are described.	Many similarities and differences between text and personal experiences are described.	Many similarities and differences between text and personal experiences are clearly described; connections are made to key elements in the text.

Name: _____ Date: _____

Rubric: Visualizing

	SKILLS	Level 1	Level 2	Level 3	Level 4
Oral Language	**Use oral language to communicate mental images.**	Rarely articulates the mental images constructed while listening.	Somewhat articulates the mental images constructed while listening.	Effectively articulates the mental images constructed while listening.	Vividly articulates the mental images constructed while listening.
	Effectively create mental images while listening.	Few images from the text are clearly represented with illustrations.	Illustrations somewhat represent images conveyed in the text.	Illustrations clearly represent ideas conveyed in the text.	Illustrations clearly represent ideas conveyed in the text; some evidence may be included to support the student's thinking.
Independent Reading	**Use imagery from the text to create visual images (illustrations).**	Few images from the text are clearly represented with illustrations and ideas.	Illustrations and ideas somewhat represent images conveyed in the text.	Illustrations and ideas clearly represent images conveyed in the text.	Illustrations and ideas clearly represent images conveyed in the text; some evidence may be included to support the student's thinking.
	Identify sensory words and images while reading.	Few sensory words and images are included.	Some sensory words and images are included.	Sensory words, phrases, and images are included.	Many sensory words, phrases, and images are included.

Name: _____   Date: _____

Rubric: Asking Questions

	SKILLS	Level 1	Level 2	Level 3	Level 4
Oral Language	**Record areas of curiosity or confusion while listening to oral texts.**	Student rarely reflects on his/her own understanding of oral texts and rarely records areas of confusion or curiosity.	Student sometimes reflects on his/her own understanding of oral texts and records areas of confusion or curiosity.	Student effectively reflects on his/her own understanding of oral texts and records areas of confusion or curiosity.	Student consistently reflects on his/her own understanding of oral texts and records areas of confusion or curiosity.
	Listen to information presented in oral texts and share questions pertaining to the text.	Student is beginning to listen attentively to oral texts, and to formulate and share questions pertaining to the text.	Student usually listens attentively to oral texts, and formulates and shares questions pertaining to the text.	Student listens attentively to oral texts, and formulates and shares questions pertaining to the text.	Student consistently listens attentively to oral texts, and formulates and shares questions pertaining to the text.
	Demonstrate respect for the ideas of peers.	Respect is rarely shown by listening to the ideas of peers and by responding with appropriate feedback.	Respect is sometimes shown by listening to the ideas of peers and occasionally responding appropriately with positive feedback.	Respect is shown by listening attentively to the ideas of peers and responding appropriately with positive feedback.	Respect is shown by listening attentively to the ideas of peers and responding appropriately with positive feedback; ideas of peers are sometimes considered as a basis for new questions about the text.
Independent Reading	**Formulate questions to initiate dialogue with a text.**	Few questions are recorded while reading text.	Some questions are recorded while reading text.	Many questions are recorded while reading text.	Many thoughtful questions are recorded while reading text.
	Ask questions before, during, and after reading a variety of texts.	Few questions are recorded at different stages of reading.	Some questions are recorded at various stages of reading.	Many questions are recorded at various stages of reading.	Many creative questions are recorded at various stages of reading.
	Ask questions and formulate answers using information from the text.	Student is beginning to reflect on questions recorded while reading and to consider answers to these questions using information from the text and his/her own ideas.	Student occasionally reflects on questions recorded while reading and considers answers to these questions using information from the text and his/her own ideas.	Student reflects on questions recorded while reading and considers answers to these questions using information from the text and his/her own ideas.	Student independently reflects on questions recorded while reading and considers answers to these questions using information from the text and his/her own ideas.

Name: _____ Date: _____

Rubric: Synthesizing

	SKILLS	Level 1	Level 2	Level 3	Level 4
Oral Language	**Create and use notes to retell the main ideas of a text.**	Few main ideas recorded while listening to the text; retell of text is simple, brief, or inaccurate.	Some main ideas recorded while listening to the text; student uses his/her notes to retell text.	Main ideas recorded while listening to the text; student uses his/her notes effectively to retell text.	Main ideas consistently recorded while listening to text; student uses his/her notes creatively to retell text.
	Identify ways in which ideas have changed while listening to a text.	Student identifies few ideas generated while listening to the text; finds it challenging to describe ways in which his/her thinking has changed.	Student identifies some ideas generated while listening to the text; is beginning to describe ways in which his/her thinking has changed.	Student identifies a number of different ideas generated while listening to the text; is able to describe ways in which his/her thinking has changed.	Student clearly identifies a number of different ideas generated while listening to the text; is able to consistently describe ways in which his/her thinking has changed.
Independent Reading	**Summarize the main ideas of a text.**	Summary may omit the main ideas or demonstrate limited understanding of the text.	Main ideas of the text are somewhat summarized.	Main ideas of the text are clearly summarized.	Main ideas of the text are clearly summarized; student's own thoughts/ideas/ opinions are added to the summary.
	Identify ways in which thoughts have developed while reading a text.	Student identifies few ideas generated while reading the text; finds it challenging to describe ways in which thinking has changed.	Student identifies some ideas generated while reading the text; is beginning to describe ways in which his/her thinking has changed.	Student identifies a number of different ideas generated while reading the text; is able to describe ways in which his/her thinking has changed.	Student clearly identifies a number of different ideas generated while reading the text; is able to consistently describe ways in which his/her thinking has changed.
	Combine important ideas from the text with own thinking to form a greater understanding of the text.	Ideas may be copied from the text and/or not combined with the student's own thinking; student demonstrates a limited understanding of the text.	Important ideas from the text are somewhat combined with the student's own thinking; student demonstrates a satisfactory understanding of the text.	Important ideas from the text are combined with the student's own thinking; student demonstrates a good understanding of the text.	Many important ideas from the text are creatively combined with the student's own thinking; student demonstrates a thorough understanding of the text.

Name: _____ Date: _____

Rubric: Integrated Metacognition

	SKILLS	Level 1	Level 2	Level 3	Level 4
Oral Language	**Identify and describe how a variety of strategies were used to interpret oral texts.**	Few strategies to interpret oral texts are identified and used; student demonstrates a limited understanding of metacognitive strategies and their uses.	Some strategies to interpret oral texts are identified and somewhat used; student demonstrates a satisfactory understanding of metacognitive strategies and their uses.	Strategies to interpret oral texts are clearly identified and used; student demonstrates a good understanding of metacognitive strategies and their uses.	Strategies to interpret oral texts are clearly identified and used; student demonstrates a thorough understanding of metacognitive strategies and their uses.
	Use a variety of strategies while listening to interpret, analyze, and connect with oral texts.	Few strategies are used while listening; student demonstrates a limited understanding of the text.	Some strategies are used to strengthen understanding while listening; student demonstrates a satisfactory understanding of the text.	Many strategies are effectively used to strengthen understanding while listening; student demonstrates a good understanding of the text.	Many strategies are effectively used to strengthen understanding while listening; student demonstrates a thorough understanding of the text.
Independent Reading	**Use a variety of strategies while reading to strengthen understanding of texts.**	Few strategies are used while reading; student demonstrates a limited understanding of the text.	Some strategies are used to strengthen understanding while reading; student demonstrates a satisfactory understanding of the text.	Many strategies are used to strengthen understanding while reading; student demonstrates a good understanding of the text.	Many strategies are effectively used to strengthen understanding while reading; student demonstrates a thorough understanding of the text.
	Identify strategies used to effectively interpret texts.	Student demonstrates a limited understanding of metacognitive strategies and is beginning to use them to interpret texts when reading.	Student demonstrates a satisfactory understanding of metacognitive strategies and somewhat uses them to interpret texts when reading.	Student demonstrates a good understanding of metacognitive strategies and uses them to interpret texts when reading.	Student demonstrates a thorough understanding of metacognitive strategies and consistently uses them to interpret texts when reading.

Class Tracking: Making Inferences

Student Names	Oral Language			Independent Reading			Observations Student's application of strategy Individual strengths or areas of need Recommendations for further instruction	Oral Language Overall	Independent Reading Overall
	Make inferences about oral texts using stated and implied ideas from the texts as evidence.	Consider the ideas of others while making inferences and drawing conclusions.	Evaluate oral texts using the ideas presented in the texts.	Identify theme or main idea of the texts.	Use evidence from the texts to infer the feelings/emotions of characters.	Identify the point of view presented in the texts and suggest some possible alternative perspectives.			

Class Tracking: Making Predictions

Student Names	Oral Language			Independent Reading			Observations Student's application of strategy Individual strengths or areas of need Recommendations for further instruction	Oral Language Overall	Independent Reading Overall
	Apply listening strategies effectively to make predictions while listening.	Revise predictions as new information is heard.	Evaluate predictions as new information is presented.	Make reasonable predictions based on evidence presented in the text.	Reassess predictions as new information is read.	Provide evidence from the text to support predictions.			

Class Tracking: Determining Important Ideas

Student Names	Oral Language		Independent Reading			Observations — Student's application of strategy — Individual strengths or areas of need — Recommendations for further instruction	Oral Language Overall	Independent Reading Overall
	Listen critically to gather information from a variety of sources.	Reflect on learning/thinking while listening.	Identify important information, ideas, and supporting details in texts.	Sequence important information, ideas, and supporting details in texts.	Summarize important ideas.			

Class Tracking: Making Connections

Student Names	Oral Language		Independent Reading			Observations Student's application of strategy Individual strengths or areas of need Recommendations for further instruction	Oral Language Overall	Independent Reading Overall
	Record a variety of connections while listening to oral text.	Demonstrate respect for peers while listening to the ideas of others.	Record text-to-text, text-to-self, and text-to-world connections.	Use personal experiences to form connections to a variety of texts.	Identify similarities and differences between texts and personal experience.			

Class Tracking: Visualizing

Student Names	Oral Language		Independent Reading		Observations Student's application of strategy Individual strengths or areas of need Recommendations for further instruction	Oral Language Overall	Independent Reading Overall
	Use oral language to communicate mental images.	Effectively create mental images while listening.	Use imagery from the text to create visual images (illustrations).	Identify sensory words and images while reading.			

Class Tracking: Asking Questions

Student Names	Oral Language			Independent Reading			Observations Student's application of strategy Individual strengths or areas of need Recommendations for further instruction	Oral Language Overall	Independent Reading Overall
	Record areas of curiosity or confusion while listening to oral texts.	Listen to information presented in oral texts and share questions pertaining to the text.	Demonstrate respect for the ideas of peers.	Formulate questions to initiate dialogue with a text.	Ask questions before, during, and after reading a variety of texts.	Ask questions and formulate answers using information from the text.			

Class Tracking: Synthesizing

Student Names	Oral Language		Independent Reading			Observations	Oral Language Overall	Independent Reading Overall
	Create and use notes to retell the main ideas of a text.	Identify ways in which ideas have changed while listening to a text.	Summarize the main idea of the text.	Identify ways in which thoughts have developed while reading a text.	Combine important ideas from the text with own thinking to form a greater understanding of the text.	Student's application of strategy / Individual strengths or areas of need / Recommendations for further instruction		

Class Tracking: Integrated Metacognition

Student Names	Oral Language		Independent Reading		Observations Student's application of strategy Individual strengths or areas of need Recommendations for further instruction	Oral Language Overall	Independent Reading Overall
	Identify and describe how a variety of strategies were used to interpret oral texts.	Use a variety of strategies while listening to interpret, analyze, and connect with oral texts.	Use a variety of strategies while reading to strengthen understanding of texts.	Identify strategies used to effectively interpret texts.			

References

Abromitis, B. (1994) "The Role of Metacognition in Reading Comprehension: Implications for Instruction" *Literacy Research and Reports*, Number 19.

Altman, Linda (1993) *Amelia's Road.* New York, NY: Lee and Low.

Anderson, N. (2003) *Metacognitive Reading Strategies Increase L2 Performance.* The Language Teacher: JALT.

Anderson, R.C., Hiebert, E.H., Scott, J.A. and Wilkinson, J. (1985) *Becoming a Nation of Readers: The report of the commission on reading.* Urbana, IL: Centre for the Study of Reading.

Ausubel, D.P. (1960) "The use of advance organizers in the learning and retention of meaningful verbal material" *Journal of Educational Psychology,* 51, 267–272.

Avi (1995) *Poppy.* New York, NY: Harper Collins.

Avi (2004) *End of the Beginning.* New York, NY: Harcourt Children's Books.

Baillie, Allan (1994) *Rebel.* New York, NY: Houghton Mifflin.

Barry, Meg (2001) *My Home Is Just Right For Me.* Toronto, ON: Scholastic Canada.

Baylor, Byrd (1986) *I'm In Charge of Celebrations.* New York, NY: Atheneum.

Baylor, Byrd (1998) *The Table Where Rich People Sit.* New York, NY: Aladdin.

Bennett, B. and Rolheiser, C. (2001) *Beyond Monet, The Artful Science of Instructional Integration.* Toronto, ON: Bookation Inc.

Berger, Barbara (1984) *Grandfather Twilight.* New York, NY: Philomel.

Berger M. and G. (2002) *Bees.* New York, NY: Scholastic.

Berger M. and G. (2002) *Turtles.* New York, NY: Scholastic.

Block, C. (2006) *Quotes to Inspire Great Reading Teachers: A Reflective Tool for Advancing Students' Literacy.* California, CA: Corwin.

Bogart, Jo Ellen (1999) *Jeremiah Learns to Read.* Toronto, ON: Scholastic Canada.

Bourgeois, Paulette (1993) *Franklin Is Bossy.* Toronto, ON: Kids Can Press.

Brashares, Ann (2003) *The Sisterhood of the Traveling Pants.* New York, NY: Delacorte.

Brinckloe, Julie (1986) *Fireflies.* Minneapolis, MN: Tandem Library.

Bromley, K., Irwin-DeVitis, L. and Modlo, M. (1995) *Graphic Organizers.* New York, NY: Scholastic Professional Books.

Brown, A., Armbruster, B.B. and Baker, L. (1986) "The role of metacognition in reading and studying" in J. Orasanu, *Reading Comprehension: From research to practice.* Hillsdale, NJ: Erlbaum.

Bunting, Eve (1991) *Fly Away Home.* New York, NY: Clarion.

Bunting, Eve (1994) *Smokey Night.* New York, NY: Harcourt Children's Books.

Bunting, Eve (1998) *Going Home.* New York, NY: HarperTrophy.

Bunting, Eve (2001) *Dandelion.* San Diego, CA: Voyager.

Canfield, Jack (1997) *Chicken Soup for the Teenager's Soul.* Florida: Health Communications Inc.

Centre for Media Literacy (2002–2007) *Empowerment for Education. Five Key Questions of Media Literacy*

Chall, Marsha Wilson (1992) *Up North at the Cabin.* New York, NY: HarperCollins.

Costa, A.L. (1991) "Mediating the metacognitive" in A. L. Costa, *The school as a home for the mind.* Palating, IL: Skylight.

Dahl, R. (1961) *James and the Giant Peach.* New York, NY: Puffin.

Danzinger, P. (1999) *I Amber Brown.* New York, NY: Scholastic.

Demi (1996) *The Empty Pot.* New York, NY: Henry Holt.

dePaola, Tomie (1979) *Oliver Button is a Sissy.* New York, NY: Harcourt Brace.

Diller, D. (2003). *Literacy Work Stations: Making Centers Work.* Portland, ME: Stenhouse.

Duffy, G.G., Roehler L.R. and Hermann, B.A. (1988) "Modeling mental processes helps poor readers become strategic readers" *The Reading Teacher,* 41, 762–767.

DuPrau, Jeanne (2003) *The City of Ember.* New York, NY: Random House.

Ellis, D. (2000) *The Breadwinner.* Toronto, ON: Groundwood.

Ellis, G. (1999) "Developing Metacognitive Awareness – The Missing Dimension" *The Journal* No. 10, April.

EnchantedLearning.com

Etools4education.com

Fletcher, Ralph (1997) *Twilight Comes Twice.* New York, NY: Clarion.

Fountas, Irene C. and Pinnell, Gay Su (2001) *Guiding Readers and Writers.* Portsmouth, NH: Heinemann.

Fowler, Allan (1992) *Frogs and Toads and Tadpoles too.* Chicago, IL: Children's Press.

Fox, M. (1994) *Koala Lou.* San Diego, CA: Voyager.

Frank, Anne (1952) *The Diary of Anne Frank.* New York, NY: Doubleday.

Funke, Cornelia (2003) *Inkheart.* New York, NY: Scholastic.

Garland, Sherry (1997) *The Lotus Seed.* San Diego, CA: Voyager.

Gear, Adrienne (2006) *Reading Power.* Markham, ON: Pembroke.

Gilman, P. (1994) *Jillian Jiggs to the Rescue.* Richmond Hill, ON: Scholastic.

Golden Gelman, Rita (1976) *Why Can't I Fly?* New York, NY: Scholastic.

Hall, T. and Strangman, N. (2002) *Graphic organizers.* Wakefield, MA: National Center on Accessing the General Curriculum. Retrieved May 2007 from http://www.cast.org/publications/ncac/ncac_go.html

Harvey, S. and Goudvis, A. (2000) *Strategies That Work: Teaching Comprehension to Enhance Understanding.* Markham, ON: Pembroke.

Henkes, Kevin (1996) *Chrysanthemum.* Westport, CT: HarperTrophy.

Hoffman, Mary (1991) *Amazing* Grace. New York, NY: Scholastic.

Houston, Gloria (1992) *My Great Aunt Arizona.* New York, NY: HarperCollins.

Israel, S., Block, C., Bauserman, K. and Kinnucan-Welsch, K. (2005) *Metacognition in Literacy Learning: Theory, Assessment, Instruction, and Professional Development.* Mahwah, NJ: Erlbaum.

Kelly, J. (2004) *The Mystery of Eatum Hall.* Cambridge, MA: Candlewick Press.

Larsen K. (2002) *The Rise and Fall of the Kate Empire.* New York, NY: Disney Press.

Lenz, K. (2005) "An Introduction to Reading Comprehension" *Special Connections,* University of Kansas.

Levine, Ellen (1989) *I Hate English.* New York, NY: Scholastic.

Levy, E. (1995) *The Snack Attack Mystery.* New York, NY: Scholastic.

Lionni, Leo (1990) *The Alphabet Tree.* New York, NY: Dragonfly.

Lobel, Arnold (1970. *Frog and Toad are Friends.* New York, NY: HarperTrophy.

Lottridge, Celia Barker (1989) *The Name of the Tree.* Toronto, ON: Groundwood.

Lowry, L (1989) *Number the Stars.* New York, NY: Doubleday.

Martin, A. (1992) *Karen's Tea Party.* New York, NY: Scholastic.

Martin, R. (1992) *The Rough Faced Girl.* New York, NY: Putnam Juvenile.

Mayer, R. (2002) *The Promise of Educational Psychology.* NJ: Pearson Education.

Mazer, A (1994) *The Salamander Room.* New York, NY: Dragonfly.

McLaughlin M. and DeVoogd, G. (2004) *Critical Literacy: Enhancing Students' Comprehension of Text.* New York, NY: Scholastic.

Miller, Debbie (2002) *Reading With Meaning: Teaching Comprehension in the Primary Grades.* Portland, ME: Stenhouse

Mills, Lauren (1991) *The Rag Coat.* Boston. MA : Little Brown.

Ontario Ministry of Education (2006) *The Ontario Curriculum: Language*

Palinscar A.S. and Ransom, K. (1988) "From the mystery spot to the thoughtful spot: The instruction of metacognitive strategies" *The Reading Teacher,* 41, 784–789.

Paris, S.G. and Jacobs, J.E. (1984) "The Benefits of Informed Instruction for Children's Reading Awareness and Comprehension Skills" *Child Development,* Vol. 55, No. 6, 2083–2093.

Paris, S.G., Lipson, M.Y. and Wixon, K.K. (1983) "Becoming a strategic reader" *Contemporary Educational Psychology,* 8, 293–316.

Pearson, P.D. and Camperell, K. (1985)."Comprehension of text structures" 323–342 in H. Singer and R.B. Rudell , *Theoretical models and processes of reading.* Newark, DE: International Reading Association.

Pfister, Markus (1992) *The Rainbow Fish.* New York, NY: NorthSouth.

Polacco, P. (1991) *Some Birthday.* New York, NY: Aladdin.

Polacco, P. (1998) *Thank You Mr. Falker.* New York, NY: Philomel.

Polacco, Patricia (2001) *The Keeping Quilt.* New York, NY: Aladdin.

Rawls, W. (1961). *Where the Red Fern Grows.* New York, NY: Random House.

Recorvits, H. (2003) *My Name is Yoon.* New York, NY: Frances Foster Books.

Rylant, Cynthia (1993) *The Relatives Came.* Point Plains, NY: Aladdin.

Seuss, T. S. G. (1968) *Horton Hatches the Egg.* New York, NY: Random House.

Seuss, T. S. G. (1971) *The Lorax.* New York, NY: Random House.

Seuss, T. S. G. (1961/1989) *The Sneetches and Other Stories.* New York, NY: Random House.

Share, J., Jolls, T. and Thoman, E. (2005) *Five Key Questions That Can Change the World: Classroom Avtivities for Media Literacy,* Center for Media Literacy.

Simon, James (1996) *Dear Mr. Blueberry.* New York, NY: Aladdin.

Singhal, Meena (2001) "Reading Proficiency, Reading Strategies, Metacognitive Awareness and L2 Readers" *The Reading Matrix* Vol. 1, No. 1, April.

Smith, Annette (1998) *Puss-In-Boots.* Richmond Hill, ON: Scholastic Canada.

Smith, M. C. (1991) "Activating implicit theories of reading: A metacognitive approach" 19–27 in T.V. Rasinski, N.D. Padak and J. Logan, *Reading is Knowledge.* Pittsburg, KS: College Reading Association.

Sorrentino, Scott (2000) *Dinosaur: a junior novel.* New York, NY: Disney Press.

Spinelli, Jerry (2003) *Loser.* New York, NY: HarperTrophy.

Steig, William (1971) *Amos and Boris.* New York, NY: Sunburst.

Steig, William (1982) *Dr. DeSoto.* New York, NY: Sunburst.

Steig, William (1986) *Brave Irene.* New York, NY: Sunburst.

Turner, Ann (2000) *Grasshopper Summer.* New York , NY: Aladdin.

Van Allsburg, Chris (1986) *The Stranger.* New York, NY: Houghton Mifflin.

Van Allsburg, Chris (1992) *The Widow's Broom.* New York, NY: Houghton Mifflin.

Van Allsburg, Chris (1993) *The Sweetest Fig.* New York, NY: Houghton Mifflin.

Van Allsburg, Chris (1994) *Bad Day at Riverbend.* New York, NY: Houghton Mifflin.

Viorst, Judith (1989) *Alexander and the Terrible, Horrible, No Good, Very Bad Day.* New York, NY: Aladdin.

Walters, Eric (1999) *Tiger by the Tail.* Toronto, ON: Dundurn Press.

Watt, Melanie (2006) *Scaredy Squirrel.* Toronto, ON: Kids Can.

Wells, Rosemary (1992) *Hazel's Amazing Mother.* New York, NY: Puffin.

Wells, Rosemary (1994) *Night Sounds, Morning Colors.* New York, NY: Penguin.

White, E.B. (1952) *Charlotte's Web.* New York, NY: HarperCollins.

Wilder, Laura Ingalls (1932) *Little House in the Big Woods.* New York, NY: HarperCollins.

Wyeth, S. (1998) *Something Beautiful.* New York, NY: Dragonfly.

Yolen, Jane (1995) *Mother Earth, Father Sky.* Honesdale, PA: Boyds Mills Press.

Yolen, Jane (2000) *Color Me a Rhyme.* Honesdale, PA: Boyds Mills Press.

Zolotow, Charlotte (2002) *If You Listen.* Philadelphia, PA: Running Press Kids.

Index